Quilt *of* Joy

Books by Mary Tatem

Quilt of Joy
Quilt of Faith
The Quilt of Hope
The Quilt of Life
The Quilt of Life: Gift Edition
A Scrapbook of Life
Just Call Me Mom

Quilt *of* Joy

STORIES OF HOPE FROM THE PATCHWORK LIFE

MARY TATEM

Revell

a division of Baker Publishing Group
Grand Rapids, Michigan

Published by Revell
a division of Baker Publishing Group
P.O. Box 6287, Grand Rapids, MI 49516-6287
www.revellbooks.com

Printed in the United States of America

Library of Congress Cataloging-in-Publication Data
Tatem, Mary.
    Quilt of joy : stories of hope from the patchwork life / Mary Tatem.
        p.   cm.
    ISBN 978-0-8007-3364-3 (pbk.)
    1. Quiltmakers—Prayers and devotions. 2. Christian women—
Prayers and devotions. I. Title.
BV4596.N44T38 2010
242'.643—dc22   2009051839

Unless otherwise indicated, Scripture is taken from GOD'S WORD®, a copy-
righted work of God's Word to the Nations. Quotations are used by permission.
Copyright 1995 by God's Word to the Nations. All rights reserved.

Scripture marked KJV is taken from the King James Version of the Bible.

Scripture marked NASB is taken from the New American Standard Bible®,
Copyright © 1960, 1962, 1963, 1968, 1971, 1972, 1973, 1975, 1977, 1995 by
The Lockman Foundation. Used by permission.

Published in association with the literary agent Janet Kobobel Grant, Books
& Such, 4788 Carissa Ave., Santa Rosa, California 95405.

    11   12   13   14   15   16   7   6   5   4   3   2

To my grandchildren—
Elizabeth, Amy, Daniel, Sharon, and Stephen Tatem
David, Heather, Holly, and Catherine Tatem
Kaitlyn, Nathan, and Thomas Tatem
Stephanie Moberg, Emily Moberg Block and Aaron
Block, Kathleen Moberg Vogel and Eric Vogel.
You each bring great joy and bright light to the pattern
of my life. I rejoice for the touch of God I see in each
of your lives. May God plant his special purposes and
dreams in your souls and anoint you to fulfill them.
God bless you.

Contents

Introduction

When I see a pretty quilt, I feel the tug of the past. I like to think I probably share some of the same hopes, dreams, and heartaches with whoever pieced and stitched together all the lovely scraps and strips of cloth. A quilt spurs me to look at my life and wonder how God can take all the torn pieces and fit them together to form a worthwhile pattern.

Before I begin a quilt I look through my cloth scraps, browse in a fabric store, and leaf through pattern books to plan and dream about the outcome I want to achieve. I find encouragement in knowing that when God created me, he planned me with even more care and foresight. He knew just which materials, relationships, and patterns to use to fulfill his purposes for me. Aren't we glad our creator never loses interest in us, his creation? He hears my cries and yours. He stitches the pieces of our lives into a lovely coverlet that brings beauty to our world.

I rejoice over the many reports of how my book *Beautiful Threads*—now reissued under the title *Quilt of Faith: Stories of Comfort from the Patchwork Life*—has touched hearts and encouraged lives with stories of God's love and concern for us.

Quilt of Joy offers more inspiring stories involving quilts. Each story carries a life lesson to enlarge your appreciation of God's great love—to reveal a little of his amazing interest in us and his desire to bring blessing to our lives.

The same artist whose lovely illustrations warmed the pages of *Beautiful Threads* once again illustrates this book with twelve more quilts to help us picture the design in the four stories that follow each drawing.

I hope *Quilt of Joy* helps you bask in the love of God, finding comfort and joy because you see God here. Most of these stories are based on real life happenings. Some of the stories come from my good friends; others come from quilt festivals and quilting guilds around the country, where I listened to quilters tell about their experiences with quilts. Yet others came from the seeds I found in historical stories buried amidst quilt instruction books. All these stories reassure us of the faithfulness of God.

Wrap up in a quilt and warm yourself in the comfort of God's love. Enjoy the fun and inspiration of how God works in our lives.

Pickle Dish

Women often use ordinary items in their life as the basis of their quilt patterns: a wrench, flowers, or the special dishes on their tables. The cut glass dishes popular between the late eighteenth and early twentieth centuries inspired the Pickle Dish pattern.

This pattern requires a lot of cutting, piecing, and stitching together of many small triangles to give the distinctive cut glass edge to the repetitive design. Some of the first Pickle Dish quilts used red and white colored designs. In our early history, spinning, weaving, and sewing occupied a great deal of even an affluent woman's time and there was an element of status to own this labor-intensive pattern.

Sleeping Stitches

"Get!" Ford ordered the Boston terrier off of the Lazy Boy chair. He rolled up his newspaper and waved it in the dog's direction to emphasize his command.

Spotty stretched but didn't jump off the chair.

"Down!" Ford swatted Spotty's backside. "Dogs don't belong on the furniture."

"Be gentle." Elaine picked up the dog. "You'd think you didn't like our puppy."

"Truth is I don't have much use for dogs. They're nothing but a nuisance." Ford sat down and shoved the lever to recline in his chair.

Elaine turned her head as Spotty tried to lick his rescuer's face.

Ford grimaced. "Gross! He's an unsanitary nuisance. Don't let him get by with all that licking stuff."

Elaine cradled the puppy in her arms. "Never mind, Spotty, Mamma loves you." She took a dog treat out of the jar on the coffee table. "Daddy-O thinks he has to act macho." She fed the dog two treats before she fired off a question to Ford. "If you dislike dogs so much, why did you let me get a puppy? I asked you before I answered the ad in the paper and brought Spotty home."

Ford only grunted behind his newspaper.

Elaine picked up the remote control for the TV and changed the channel from the basketball game to a cooking show.

"Hey, I'm watching the game," Fred objected.

"You're reading the newspaper," Elaine corrected.

"I can listen to the sports announcer and read the paper at the same time."

"And here I thought only women could multitask," Elaine said, but she laughed and switched the channel back to the game. "Who's winning?" she asked Fred, trying to start a conversation.

"You don't even know who's playing who." Ford didn't lower the paper.

Elaine sighed, picked up the novel she was reading, and settled on the sofa with Spotty on her lap.

Later that evening, Elaine looked at Ford dozing in the recliner. "Are you asleep?" she asked, then shrugged when he didn't answer. "Guess so. Happy dreams, sweetheart." Elaine headed upstairs to bed. A cluck of her tongue brought Spotty behind her. With the help of a nearby stool, the puppy scrambled onto the bed. When Elaine climbed into bed she rested a hand on the sleeping terrier curled up beside her. "Dreaming of climbing a tree and catching a squirrel?" she asked, patting Spotty's back. He stopped twitching as Elaine stroked his back and soon his snorts turned back to gentle, rhythmic breathing. Elaine pulled the blue and white Pickle Dish quilt up over her shoulders and Spotty. They snuggled.

Sleep still eluded her when Ford came upstairs. She listened to the sounds of his preparation for bed. When he turned on the electric toothbrush, she smiled because she knew that was the sound of Ford's last bedtime ritual. Elaine closed her eyes and pretended to be asleep.

Sure enough, Ford soon padded into the bedroom, turned back the covers on his side of the bed, and pulled Spotty along with the Pickle Dish quilt onto his pillow. "Sugar puppy," he whispered, "I love you. Curl up with Daddy-O and have sweet doggie dreams." Ford began to kiss the puppy.

The sound of smooches was too much for Elaine. She abandoned her pretense at sleep and burst out laughing. "A nuisance, huh?" She picked Spotty up and plopped him at their feet. "Woof, woof," she said, snuggling up to her husband, throwing the Pickle Dish quilt over his head. "How about an 'I love you' for me too?"

     ## The Master Pattern

> God made every type of wild animal, every type of domestic animal, and every type of creature that crawls on the ground. God saw that they were good.
>
> Genesis 1:25

God made animals not only to provide for the needs of mankind but to delight us. Watching the antics of a pet, seeing the grace of a wild gazelle, observing the beauty of a tropical bird each in its own way reveals a bit of the magnitude and scope of God's power.

Since we know the pleasure we feel when someone admires one of our children, we can believe it pleases God when we take pleasure in an animal he created. We don't need to feel embarrassed at the affection we feel for our pets; kindness to animals is a hallmark of a good civilization.

How much more, then, must God take pleasure when we enjoy the people he created. How we treat other people must rank much higher to God because people are made in his image. Grown people need affection and attention as much as pets and children. Elaine's good nature tolerated Ford's efforts to hide his true feelings. Putting our affection into words for those we love meets a basic hunger in our loved one.

Prayer: God, give me an appreciation for each person. Help me see and treat every individual as your creation. Help me overcome any reluctance to express my affection to my loved ones. Help me have patience with those who find it difficult to express love.

Quilted Protection

"Blake, I need to open the chest one more time." Amanda clutched the framed family portrait, then turned toward her husband who stood checking the knots that secured the chicken cage onto the back of the covered wagon. The draft horses, Salt and Pepper, shifted in their harnesses. "I want to tuck this portrait inside the Pickle Dish quilt to protect the glass over it. We'll bounce a lot on the trail to Oklahoma."

Blake hesitated. "You mean the Red and White quilt? Isn't that quilt already wrapped around all your china plates?"

"There's room for one more thing in the top fold," Amanda told Blake, then turned to her father. "This is the most important memento we're taking. Here I thought the autographs on the Pickle Dish quilt would be my visible reminder of family back here, but a real picture is even better." Amanda tried to smile at her father. "Thanks, Papa."

Blake took the picture and climbed into the back of the wagon. Amanda stood on tiptoes and leaned into the round opening of the canvas wagon cover to make certain her treasure was stored safely.

Climbing down, Blake announced, "It's time."

With a flurry of calico skirts, Amanda's sisters surrounded her, reaching up for hugs.

"I don't think I can let go," Sally said, clinging.

"Me neither." Elizabeth moved over to make room for their mother.

With a sob, Mother buried her head into her daughter's shoulder. Amanda lowered her face until their tears mixed on their cheeks. She tried listening to the blowing sounds from the draft horses behind her to help her regain control.

Blake cleared his throat and shuffled his feet. The horses stomped flies off their legs. "The horses are getting restless," Blake said. The sound of jingling metal accompanied the horses' snorts as they shook their heads.

Amanda's father stepped up to his grieving family. "They need to leave while the day is still young. They have far to go while it's still daylight." At the unnatural sound of his voice, Elizabeth allowed him to loosen her grip on her sister.

"God go with you, daughter."

Amanda turned to receive his stiff hug, an unusual expression for her father. Her mother stepped aside for his goodbye, but little Sally clung fiercely to her sister's arm.

"We'll send for you to visit when we're settled." Amanda spoke to the pain in her mother's face; she hoped, wished, but doubted she was telling her mother the truth.

Blake reached out to shake his father-in-law's hand. He put one arm around Amanda. With gentle pressure he began to lead her toward the wagon.

"No, you can't leave." Sally ran along beside her big sister, tugging at her dress.

"Hush, now, Sally." Mother held her hand firmly in her own. "Don't make it any harder for your sister."

"Please write," Amanda called in a choked voice.

Blake slapped the reins and the horses pulled against the weight of the wagon. Pans clanged against the side of the post where they were tied. The hens in their cage squawked protest. The cow lumbered behind on his lead.

Amanda waved one hand and muffled a cry from her mouth with the other. She shifted on the wooden plank to keep her eyes on her family. She didn't turn to face forward until her dear ones disappeared behind the dust stirred up by the horses and the wagon wheels.

"What an exciting adventure we begin." Blake reached over to squeeze Amanda's hand. "It's the dream of a lifetime." His heart swelled with dreams of opportunity for their family's future.

Amanda allowed her hand to lie in his, but she couldn't squeeze back. Her heart squeezed instead. She dreaded the hardships and loneliness that lay ahead.

 ## The Master Pattern

> Lo, I am with you always even unto the end of the world.
>
> Matthew 28:20 KJV

No matter how bereft or alone we feel or how upside down our world seems, this verse along with Hebrews 13:5 brings comfort: "I will never abandon you or leave you." We know that in the midst of the most heart-wrenching separations, sorrows, or dangers Jesus is with us, covering us in his love like the warmest of quilts.

Prayer: God, make your presence real to me in the hard places of my life.

Ruined Quilt

"No chips," June yelled before the baseball game began on the street in front of her public housing development. She threw an old Help Wanted sign onto the street for second base.

"You'd better yell 'no chips' too," June told her new neighbor Rosy, who had just moved into the apartment above hers.

"Why?" Rosy sat on the curb to fix her shoestring by tying a knot where it had broken. "You don't like potato chips?"

"Not that kind of chips. If you forget to yell 'no chips' before we start our game, and we break a window with our ball, then the ones who forget to yell 'no chips' have to chip in to pay for the window, which is expensive. New windows cost seventy-five cents."

"Seventy-five cents!" Rosy frowned and quickly yelled, "No chips." She turned to June. "I didn't know it cost so much to replace a window. Maybe I shouldn't play." She backed up the cracked sidewalk to the candy-striped doorway of the confectionary store.

"Yeah, it's expensive, and our apartments are at the end of the street where a lot of the balls go." June thumbed toward the apartment. "The window in the bedroom where we kids sleep was broken in May. Even though I yelled too, everyone remembered to yell 'no chips' so Mom and Stevie and I had to pay. Now, I don't have money to buy comic books at the candy store this summer."

"Comic books are too expensive for me too," Rosy said.

"Not at the end of the month, when the new comics come out. Mr. Goodwin tears the cover off the old ones and sells them to us kids for ten cents. That's when we buy them. Stevie likes *Tarzan* the best. My favorites are *Little Audrey* and *Nancy.* You can borrow mine."

"Thanks. Who broke your window?"

"Abe, and he can hit really far, but I'll bet no one can hit as high as your window on the second floor. You probably won't get a ball through it." June tried to reassure Rosy. "I hated when the first ball came through. All the glass fell on my Pickle Dish quilt. It was so full of little slivers, Mother was afraid I'd get cut and threw it out. I cried and cried." June closed her eyes at the memory.

"I still feel sad when I think about it. My grandma made that quilt and it helped me remember her and how she'd read Bible stories to me. Bible stories made me forget sad stuff."

"I cried when we had to move because Daddy left," Rosy said.

"I cry about my Daddy leaving sometimes too, but only in my bed at night. I used to cover my head with my quilt so Stevie wouldn't hear me. Now I just read my comics and try to laugh instead. Maybe you can laugh at my comics and not cry too."

Too late. Rosy already had tears running down her cheeks.

"Come on, Rosy. Whacking the ball as hard as you can and running top speed around the bases helps you forget the sad stuff as much as comics. I'll buy you a *Nancy* comic all your own as soon as Stevie and I pay off the window."

Rosy wiped her eyes with her hand.

"Maybe we can read Bible stories like Grandma did. Do you think that would help?"

Rosy nodded. She looked at June a long moment, then ventured, "Will you be my friend?"

June beamed. "I've always dreamed of having a friend my own age. Mostly boys live around here."

 ## The Master Pattern

A joyful heart is good medicine, but depression drains one's strength.

Proverbs 17:22

Exercise helps lift depression, and hearty laughter relieves a sad mood. The ability to look at life with a sense of humor is a skill to covet. People who can make us laugh do us a good turn. Seek friends who know how to look on life with a cheerful attitude. As long as humor is not at someone's expense, it is a great gift to others.

Prayer: God, increase my sense of humor. Help me be a cheerful and encouraging person to others.

24

Prisoner Stitches

"Mavis, make it easy on yourself," Judge Roscoe Lambert entreated his neighbor as she stood before him in his courtroom.

His wife, Edith, winced from her seat on a bench near the back of the courtroom, where she hoped Mavis wouldn't see her. Her friend stood tall before the rail which separated her from the courthouse judge. Edith could see Mavis clamp her lower lip between her teeth. *Poor thing,* Edith thought. *I'll bet she's trembling.* She felt overwhelmed with regret as she watched her husband, robed in black, exuding authority. *If his steely eyes make my stomach shrink within me, what must they do to Mavis?*

Edith hadn't visited her husband's court before, and she found it hard to identify this stern authority figure as the same man who killed the rattlesnake in Mavis's garden after her husband, Franklin, left to fight for the Rebel cause. This was the man who hired Mavis to mend his family's clothes when he knew Franklin's Confederate army wages weren't adequate for her family. If Edith didn't know her husband so well, even she could feel intimidated by Roscoe Lambert in his black robe.

"Never!" Mavis answered, interrupting Edith's thoughts. "I'll never swear allegiance to the Federal Government. My heart is firmly united with the cause of the South."

"Mavis, think about your stance. It's a lost cause." The judge passed a hand over his eyes.

How had it come to this? Neighbor against neighbor in this small Kentucky community. Edith remembered Franklin's passion for the Southern cause. She was at his home the day he took his rifle from its pegs over the fireplace, gathered his bag of gunpowder, swung his heavy coat over his shoulder, and kissed Mavis goodbye to fight for Southern secession. Shouts of anger and derision rang out along with cheers of support and approval as the Confederate recruits left for war. Their small Kentucky town was torn asunder by conflicting loyalties, and split by opinions, passions, and convictions on both sides of the war.

Judge Lambert's clenched jaw reflected the tension in their community. His hands nervously fingered the paper before him, betraying his inner conflict for his neighbor. Before he spoke, he cleared his throat and spat in a brass spittoon.

Edith watched Mavis's anguished face across the silence of the courtroom.

"Mavis Gardener, in accordance to the laws of the United States of America, I sentence you to house arrest. You are not to leave your property until you submit to the Federal Government and swear your allegiance to her."

The judge nodded to the bailiff. "See that the deputy escorts Mrs. Gardener to her home, and place her property on your list of sites to check daily for compliance with this order." He banged his gavel down. "Next case."

The bailiff seized Mavis by the elbow and led her from the courtroom.

At the door, Edith reached out a hand to Mavis, whose eyes betrayed both pain and regret. "Can I bring you supplies?" Edith asked. "What do you need?"

"Fabric." Mavis spit out the word. "Enough for a large Pickle Dish quilt. That's an intricate enough project to pass a prisoner's time."

"What colors?" Hurt tightened Edith's lips.

"Red and white. You can skip the blue. Blood or surrender are the only choices offered to the citizens of this part of Kentucky."

Edith let her arm drop, and the bailiff escorted Mavis to a waiting wagon.

Later that day, as Edith approached the door of Mavis's home, she could see the cultivated rows of Mavis's garden. At least her friend had already planted a spring garden for provisions. Roscoe's sentence didn't say Mavis had to stay inside her house.

Edith knocked at the door. When Mavis didn't answer right away, Edith laid a bag of walnuts on the stoop along with some jars of canned beans and a bundle of material. Red and white fabric poked through the ends. Edith retreated to the gate. She looked up to see Mavis standing in the doorway.

"If you want company, I'll bring my quilt patches to work with you while you piece your Pickle Dish quilt," Edith called. "Let me know if you run out of necessities."

Mavis didn't speak. She waved, gathered the provisions, and disappeared into her home. Edith stood for a long moment, paralyzed by the loud wrenching sobs coming from behind the door. *Who would have dreamed the nation would come to such straits? Neighbors and family estranged from one another.* Edith straightened her back. A court order didn't have to sever friendships.

Another loud wail reached Edith. She hesitated another moment. Resolutely she walked back up the walk, climbed the steps, and knocked again on the door.

 ## The Master Pattern

I needed clothes, and you gave me something to wear. I was sick, and you took care of me. I was in prison, and you visited me.

Matthew 25:36

Not all prisons have bars and doors fastened with strong locks. Sometimes we find ourselves imprisoned by our emotions. Our unspoken thoughts can create a prison from which we can't find release. Whenever we help someone, whether in a literal prison or a prison of emotions, we serve Jesus. When we befriend and love people in such conditions, we love the Lord.

God is the only one who has the power to change emotional outlooks, but we can lead people to meet the Author of change: Jesus.

Prayer: Make me sensitive to perceive the locked bars of emotional prisons. Help me lead to you these people trapped by their thoughts, as you can set the prisoner free.

Pine Tree

Tree quilts date from the earliest years of our nation, and the motif appeared on flags and coins. As one of the oldest quilt motifs in America, trees are designed in many variations and known by many different names, such as the Temperance Tree and the Tree of Paradise. Often the tree trunk is appliquéd and the tree foliage is pieced from triangles.

The *Kansas City Star* printed the first published Pine Tree pattern on September 22, 1928, and offered the pattern for sale for five cents. Before magazines and newspapers began to publish patterns, they were passed from woman to woman either verbally or copied by hand on whatever paper one could find.

Math Quilts

"How did your parent-teacher conference go today?" Don asked his wife, who was busy quilting, her favorite stress buster.

"Good, I think," Barb said. "Most of the children are doing well so I wasn't worried about the conferences, except for Noah Blair. His mother was defensive at first when I explained I couldn't allow one student to disrupt a learning atmosphere. But she listened when I told her how Noah created distractions for the entire class—how during every test he bangs his ruler in a continuous drum beat on the metal legs of his chair. No one can think over the din." Barb pounded her quilting ruler against the nearby lamp base to demonstrate Noah's aggravating behavior.

"Mrs. Blair eventually agreed for us to send him to finish his test in the principal's office," Barb continued. "She also agreed that standards for Noah's classroom behavior might need to be sterner than for a student alone in his home. She volunteered to observe his study habits at home. I think she'll support me and see that I'm trying to help him."

"You won," Don said.

"Voila!" Barb said, leaning forward. "I have another winning idea—a wonderful idea, if I do say so myself. I finished it as we talked." With a flourish, she cut the last thread, stuck her needle in the pincushion, and held up her quilt for her husband to see. "Don't you think it's a perfect teaching aid for my math classes?"

"Uh . . ." Don searched for words. "I'm just a plain old guy. Fill me in on how a quilt teaches math."

"Look, the pine trees are made of triangles, the trunks are rectangles, and the pots that the trees sit in are squares. See, the borders around the pine trees contain even more geometric shapes: trapezoids, hexagons, diamonds." Barb's voice rose with enthusiasm.

"Clever," Don said, "but aren't your fourth graders beyond the study of shapes?"

"Of course, but our daughter's first grade students aren't. She plans to borrow the quilt for her class when I'm not using it to teach fractions."

"Is that why one of the pine trees is only half a tree and the next one looks like one-fourth of a tree? Maybe this one is one-third." Don pointed.

"You get an 'A.' Using the quilt as a visual aid is unusual enough to catch the kids' attention, even the daydreamers, don't you think? I intend to use it to teach area and perimeters too. The kids can measure the rectangles and multiply the base times the height to figure the rectangle area. They'll multiply one-half the base times the height to figure the area of the triangles. By the time they calculate all the different-sized triangles that represent the pine tree greenery, they should have that formula down pat. Then they can figure the angles of the triangles, the perimeter of the whole quilt, and the diameters of the circles."

"I never knew a quilt could teach so much."

"Pretty good, huh? You said you were a daydreamer when you were a boy. Do you think you would have paid attention to math, if you had this kind of an aid when you were a fourth grade boy?"

"I'm in the forty-four-year-old grade, and I sure would pay a lot of attention if my teacher was as pretty as you. Maybe you and I should measure the perimeter from underneath the quilt." Don reached out for a hug, wrinkling the quilt between them.

 ## The Master Pattern

> He asked me, "What do you see, Amos?"
> I answered, "A plumb line."
> Then the Lord said, "I'm going to hold a plumb line in the middle of my people Israel. I will no longer overlook what they have done."
>
> Amos 7:8

A plumb line is a simple tool of a weight attached to a cord or string and allowed to hang free. For centuries, carpenters and masons used the simple plumb line to mark the vertical line that helped build straight walls.

God's Word provides standards of righteousness like a plumb line to measure our behavior. Although we rejoice in God's great grace and the amazing mercy he extends toward us, we must understand that he measures our lives by his standards of righteousness. With this understanding, we live in gratitude to Jesus, who died on the cross to bear our unrighteousness so that we can enter into the presence of God without the stain of sin. Jesus took the consequences of our faults.

Knowing our inability to attain the absolute righteousness of God, it's no wonder we raise our voices to praise our God and celebrate Jesus with joyful hearts.

Prayer: God, help me follow the plumb line of your word as the standard for my life, my choices, and my decisions.

Don't Stitch Importance

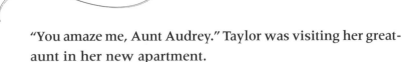

"You amaze me, Aunt Audrey." Taylor was visiting her great-aunt in her new apartment.

"Why's that?" Aunt Audrey set out teacups and cookies.

"You lost everything in your house fire, but you don't look back." Taylor helped herself to two cookies. "You don't show any regrets."

"Actually that's not entirely true. I have lots of regrets, but I don't waste them on the fire."

"Waste regrets? It seems to me that losing your house and everything in it to a fire is worthy of lots of regret."

Aunt Audrey offered Taylor a sugar cube. "I save my regrets for where I've let people down. The fire took my possessions, but that's all hay and stubble compared to people."

Taylor stirred her tea until the sugar dissolved. "I couldn't believe it when you called and said your house burned down and everything was gone. I expected to find you sobbing. You were so calm I thought you were on a tranquilizer or something."

"Surprised you, did I?"

"You've had to start all over, and you are way past middle age." Taylor bit her lip. "That didn't come out right." She felt a hot blush reach her hairline.

Aunt Audrey laughed and patted Taylor's knee. "That's all right, I *am* an old lady. Maybe that's the secret. Everything is a matter of perspective. After all these years, I look at things differently than when I was young."

"Remember when my husband died twelve years ago, sudden and unexpected? Now that was grief. Grinding, unrelenting grief." Aunt Audrey closed her eyes briefly. "What's a house and its contents compared to the loss of the love of your life? Poof! Nothing!"

"I know Uncle Will's death was terrible, but when your house burned, you lost your entire quilt collection—all those wonderful handmade quilts."

"Very unfortunate," Aunt Audrey agreed.

"Even your Pine Tree quilt was burned—your prize-winning Pine Tree quilt. The newspaper took a picture of your quilt when it won the blue ribbon."

"I was sorry to lose that, but it didn't compare to losing my William. The final truth is that people are what matter most in life. We aren't meant to hang onto things too tight. Things don't go to heaven with us. But loving people is a kind of treasure stored up for heaven. Love given and returned is the stuff of happy dreams."

Aunt Audrey picked up a sugar cube and turned it in her fingers. "Strange, but our relationships with people are our greatest source of joy and our greatest griefs." She dropped the sugar cube into Taylor's cup. "People are the sweeteners for life. People are made in the image of God,

35

and that's why they touch our hearts so deeply. I'm sorry my quilts burned, but I'm more regretful when I think of the sharp words I sometimes had with William."

Taylor shook her head. "I can't believe you ever had sharp words. You two were the picture of lovebirds."

"We loved one another, all right, but we thought we would have years and years together, so we let little things get under our skin. I wish we had lived with a more eternal perspective. We didn't have the years we expected. I regret I turned little annoyances into big aggravations."

"Oh, dear, if you regret little annoyances, you'd better pray for me, Aunt Audrey. I've been so impatient with my dad. We've had more than sharp words—shouting matches. He's so . . . so controlling. It makes me so mad." Taylor set her cup down too fast and tea sloshed up the sides, into the saucer. She grabbed her paper napkin to mop up the mess.

Aunt Audrey put her arm around Taylor's shoulders. "We'll pray. We have to rely on God's mercy to find a heavenly perspective on the trials of this life. Too often our human nature rules our reactions."

When she left her great-aunt's apartment, Taylor felt as if she had been with Jesus. She drove straight to the newspaper office to research the library archives for the picture of Aunt Audrey's prize-winning Pine Tree quilt, then she printed out a copy and put it in the mail to her aunt.

 The Master Pattern

Now if any man build upon this foundation gold, silver, precious stones, wood, hay, stubble; Every man's work shall be made manifest: for the day

36

shall declare it, because it shall be revealed by fire; and the fire shall try every man's work of what sort it is.

1 Corinthians 3:12–13 KJV

Since life is full of uncertainties, we need to seek God for the wisdom to live life with as few regrets as possible. We are imperfect and try one another's patience, yet when we show God's love to people, we build treasure in heaven. Hasty responses can set up regrets, but we will never regret kind words and acts.

Prayer: God, help our daily lives build the treasure of love and reduce the opportunities for later regrets.

Surprise

Jocelyn froze. Standing still behind a wall of fabric bolts in her local quilt shop, she thought: *That sounds like my husband's voice at the front of the store.* But it couldn't be—Jerry couldn't be here. His emphatic refusal last week to even consider buying her a new sewing machine still rankled her. He didn't understand how much time she wasted trying to get her old machine and its worn out parts to work. She argued that she could buy a new machine for the money required to fix it. Well, almost, if the repairman could find the replacement parts she needed.

She hadn't told Jerry that she planned to stop by the store to pick out fabric for her Pine Tree quilt. She felt justified in buying new material for a wide, elegant border because of her thrifty use of tiny little scraps of leftover material to cut out the small triangles for the pine trees.

But that was Jerry's voice, all right. Jocelyn put a bolt of flowered green back on the shelf and stepped toward the end of the display shelves to greet her husband.

"Help me pick out a sewing machine for my wife," he was telling Lea, the clerk.

Jocelyn stopped in disbelief.

"Don't tell my wife. I want to surprise her."

Jocelyn swallowed a gasp.

"She comes in here a lot. You probably know her, Jocelyn Stark. She's been making a quilt with a tree-like design, and she tells me her old machine keeps knotting the bobbin thread. She said the repairman could probably fix it for a hefty fee."

Jocelyn separated two bolts of fabric to peer through a tiny gap. There stood Jerry, his broad back to her and his brown hair hanging too far over his collar. *I need to cut his hair this week*, she thought.

Jerry gestured to a nearby machine. "Jocelyn told me the new machines do fancy stitches and things the old ones don't do."

"They sure do," Lea said. "Did your wife say what capabilities she wants in a machine?"

"Naw, she does a lot of quilting on her machine and mends our clothes. Makes clothes for our granddaughters' dolls too."

"Well then," Lea said, beaming, "she uses her machine enough to justify a nice, new one. Excuse me a moment, and I'll get a catalogue to give you an idea of the prices and features of the various machines."

"Can't afford every fancy gadget," Jerry called after her. "Just show me a good, serviceable machine."

"We have some nice middle-of-the-line models," Lea said as she walked behind the wall of fabric bolts.

Jocelyn put her finger to her lips as Lea rounded the wall. Lea nodded, grabbed a catalog from a small table, and pointed to the picture of a machine. Jocelyn checked the printed price, shook her head, and pointed to a less expensive one beneath it. Lea mouthed the words "good choice" and returned to Jerry.

"Look at the list of what this machine does. It's a good buy, and we have one in stock."

Jerry smiled. "That's good. Her birthday is next week. Don't tell her if she comes in here before then."

"Mum's the word," Lea smiled, her fingers crossed behind her back. "What a wonderful way to celebrate her birthday."

Jocelyn hugged herself in delight. Some dreams do come true.

 ## The Master Pattern

It is a gift from God to be able to eat and drink and experience the good that comes from every kind of hard work.

Ecclesiastes 3:13

What fun we experience when we give someone the thing that delights them! Whatever hard work is necessary to make the gift possible becomes worth the effort, when we see the joy it brings.

It is humbling to realize that God feels the same kind of delight in giving us the wide variety of blessings we enjoy in life. We please God when we acknowledge all that we eat, drink, and own comes as a gift from him. When we realize that even our ability to work hard and to enjoy good experiences are a gift from him, our gratitude enlarges our soul.

Prayer: Thank you, God, that you are the giver of all that is good in our lives. We thank you for the blessing of work, food, and drink. Grant us the ability to give good gifts to others. Help us discern when a word, a hug, or an actual present will bring gladness.

Feel the Quilt

"Barry, stop!" Rita broke into a run. She had only let go for a moment of her five-year-old's hand, to pull her door key from her purse, yet he was already tearing across the apartment grounds toward the street.

"Stop! Cars!" Rita screamed. Fear lent speed to her feet. With adrenalin-driven energy, she grabbed Barry's arm before he reached the curb.

"You must never run off like that," Rita scolded. She kept a tight hold on Barry's arm and dragged him across the tiny lawn, through the outside apartment opening, to the front door of her own apartment. While she tried to insert the key into the lock with her left hand, she looked up. Her neighbor stared down from the entryway of the apartment at the top of the steps.

God, this is too hard, Rita prayed as she put the key in her mouth and switched hands to hold her wriggling son with her left hand. She managed to open her door with her right hand and propel Barry inside. He was groaning loud, unintelligible sounds. She closed the door behind her and leaned against it, heart still pounding from her fear-driven sprint.

Back in his familiar surroundings, Barry sat down close to the television. He rocked back and forth in front of the empty screen and made contented noises.

Before she could make sure he was settled, the doorbell rang. Rita ran a sleeve across her eyes and opened the door a crack. Wilma, her neighbor from upstairs, stood outside.

Humiliated that her neighbor had witnessed this latest episode, Rita wanted to slam the door shut. She resisted the urge.

Wilma was holding out Rita's purse.

"Oh, thank you," Rita said. "I forgot I dropped it trying to get Barry before he ran into the street." Rita ran her sleeve over her eyes again. It didn't work. At the sympathetic expression on Wilma's face, tears began to run.

"My dear, how can I help?" Wilma stepped inside and closed the door behind her.

While Wilma took over the kitchen to make a pot of tea, Rita began breaking off pieces of a peanut butter sandwich for Barry, and out poured the story of Barry's descent into autism. Together the women grieved over Barry's difficulties learning basic things.

Wilma offered to babysit sometimes when Rita had a pressing errand to accomplish. Best of all, she provided a listening ear when Rita's load felt too heavy to carry.

One month later, Wilma arrived with a gift: a Pine Tree quilt.

"I've never seen a quilt like this," Rita said, when Wilma spread it over the sofa.

"Probably never will again. I made it to help teach Barry about shapes and textures."

Each pine tree was made of a different fabric. One was corduroy, one wool, another silky, yet another fuzzy like fur. A different-shaped package sat at the base of each tree: squares, triangles, rectangles, diamonds.

Barry grunted happy noises and held the gift to his face. He rubbed his lips with the silky tree and fingered the corduroy square under it. A leather angel hovered over one tree and a fluffy cloud over another. "Soft," Barry said.

Rita stared, surprised and happy. "He spoke. I've been afraid to dream he could talk."

 ## The Master Pattern

> Almighty LORD, you made heaven and earth by your great strength and powerful arm. Nothing is too hard for you.
>
> Jeremiah 32:17

Sometimes our lives contain problems that seem beyond solutions. When we run into difficult circumstances we find too hard to handle, too hard to bear, too difficult to solve, our solution is to run into the powerful arms of God. Ask him for his strength. Nothing is too hard for him, and he will supply his great strength for us to bear our trials.

We can run to him over and over, and he does not weary of hearing our pleas for strength. In fact, he is pleased we continue to seek his strength to replace our weakness.

Prayer: God, I'm throwing myself into your powerful arms. Please substitute your strength for my weakness and lift me up in my trial.

Bear Claw

Common things encountered in the early settlers' days formed the basis of many of their quilt designs. Bears were one—both a menace to animals and people living in isolated woods and a benefit as game, providing fat for lubrication, and skins for rugs on the rough, cold cabin floors of the settlers as they moved West.

When Bear Claw patterns emerged in quilts, sometimes the pattern was called Hand of Friendship or Ducks Foot in the Mud. Each paw is a square with small triangles sewn around two sides to represent a bear's claws—a popular way to use fabric scraps.

Mystery Quilt

"What's that black bag on the front porch?" Monica's husband, Larry, braked his car to a stop in front of their garage door.

"I don't know," Monica said. "Did you forget to take out the garbage this morning?"

"No, and it's been collected." Larry pointed to the sidewalk behind him. "The trash bin is on its side with the lid open. You don't suppose the city is rejecting our garbage now?" Larry's laugh sounded more rueful than merry.

"Still sore because the city refused to allow your lighthouse on the front lawn?" Monica tried to keep her voice lighthearted. She knew that it was the city's cutbacks that hurt Larry the most. After the recent budget cuts, the city contracted out Larry's job of managing the buoys in the harbor. His dreams of advancement were crushed.

"Phooey to bureaucrats," he said. "I built that model lighthouse with my own hands. It's an important symbol of my years as a waterman, and I should be able to put it where I want it. After all, I own this property." He walked up the steps and hefted the black refuse bag.

"This bag doesn't feel like garbage." Larry swung open the front door.

Monica blocked the doorway. "Let's take a look out here. If it *is* our garbage, I don't want the bag to break inside the house." Monica untied the red closure on the bag and peered inside. "It's material," she said. As she pulled out the cloth, her eyes widened with surprise. "No, it's a quilt. Hold the door open, and I'll bring it inside." Monica gathered the quilt in her arms.

Larry followed with the black bag. "Why would someone leave a quilt on our steps? Seems like an invitation for a thief."

Monica unfolded the quilt over the sofa. "It's a Bear Claw quilt. Do you think someone got the wrong house number?"

"I don't know. Did anyone tell you they had a quilt for you?" Larry asked.

"No, but the green and yellow colors match our bedroom," Monica said, spreading out the comforter to examine closer. "You know, this quilt has to be from someone who knows us. The ivy vine border stitched around the quilt border is a giveaway."

"How so?" Larry asked.

"I've always loved ivy on anything because it was my college sorority symbol."

"Why would someone go to so much trouble to make such a thoughtful gift for us and then leave it in a bag on the porch? And, by the way, the ivy may be for you, but you could say the bear claws are symbolic for my hunting."

Monica studied the pattern. "Several people have mentioned the bad timing of my retirement coming at the same time as your job cut." She turned over one corner of the quilt and smiled with satisfaction. "Ah, yes. Good. Here's a label." She read, "To Celebrate Monica Forest's retirement. Presented June 2008 by Jill Ryan in honor of our friendship."

Monica squealed. "Jill! I should have guessed. We were in the same sorority. How special! A handmade quilt with symbols important to us."

"If she likes us this much, I think I'll ask her to introduce a resolution to the neighborhood committee she chairs," Larry said, grinning. "Maybe the committee will allow me to display my lighthouse in the backyard behind our porch. No one can see that location from the street."

"Do it," Monica encouraged. "That would fulfill one of your dreams."

"That leaves the dream of having a job." A rueful tone colored Larry's voice.

"Dream about our golf dates instead," Monica said and hugged her husband.

 ## The Master Pattern

Turn all your anxiety over to God because he cares for you.

1 Peter 5:7

God knows what matters to each of us, what touches each of our hearts. He understands the essence of who each of us is and why. He cares about what is important to every person and takes pleasure in bringing joy to every soul. He knows your delights and your worries. He cares about everything.

You can trust that he sees your concerns and is able to work in every situation. He can remold your dreams until they fit his plans.

Prayer: God, thank you that you care about what is important to me. Thank you for supplying delightful moments in my life and meeting my needs.

Souvenir Fabric

"Maybe you should wait to buy souvenirs until after the ceremony in the Great Machinery Hall." Ralph cast an anxious look at the clock tower standing near Philadelphia Fairmount Park.

"I won't be long." His wife, Mabel, knew he was eager to see the Centennial Fair displays. "With this huge crowd, the best items may sell out if we wait."

"By the same token," Ralph said, "it's going to get too crowded to see well if we don't get in Machinery Hall soon. Besides, I'd like to see most of the displays before General Ulysses—oops, I mean President Grant—arrives."

Mabel was already handling the souvenirs for sale. She held up a red, white, and blue bandana flag to show her friend Helen. "Don't you think the children at the orphanage would like quilts made from these patriotic bandanas?"

"Good idea," Helen said. "Maybe a quilt would make those sad children smile and forget their heartaches for a little while. This handkerchief fabric would look good in a quilt too." Helen handed the clerk a strip of fabric with handkerchiefs printed two abreast down the length. "See, this cloth even has the date, 1876, on it. I'll buy an extra length for myself as a memento of the centennial."

Ralph sighed and fell in behind the women. "We'd better keep an eye on them, Charles," he told Helen's husband. "It would be a shame to come all this way from Virginia and miss seeing President Grant when he turns the lever on the Corliss steam engine. I hear it will power up all the machines in this building. I don't want to be standing outside the door just because we're buying patriotic doodads."

"What pattern should we use?" Helen didn't hear the men fretting over the time.

"I think four bear claws at the center of each square should be made out of red, white, and blue," Mabel said. "Then we'll figure out some kind of border." She searched inside her reticule for money to pay the clerk.

"Why not put one of these commemorative flag bandanas on each corner of the quilt?" Helen held the bandana out to Mabel. "The United States flag is colorful. See how small flags surround our flag with its thirty-six stars."

The clerk couldn't help interjecting, "Each little flag represents the countries participating in the Centennial Fair. These bandanas are selling fast."

"Perfect." Ralph reached around his wife to hand the clerk a bill. "Let's wrap this and get inside the hall." The minute the fabric was wrapped, he took his wife by the hand and led the way. The foursome entered Great Machinery Hall. Even Mabel fell silent when she spotted the giant steam engine towering above them.

Ralph took advantage of the silence. He was ready to talk about anything but quilts.

He read a sign aloud: "The Corliss is forty feet high and weighs seven hundred tons."

"What power," Charles said, tipping back his head for a good look.

"The power of 2,500 horses are wrapped up in that machine," Ralph said. "Hook up that monster to anything that needs hauling away, and it's going to move things."

Helen tried steering their group to another area. "I hear there are sewing machines and machines to spin cotton here too," she said.

"Imagine how fast you could do your sewing and mending, Helen, with a sewing machine." Charles nudged his wife.

"You'd love a sewing machine, wouldn't you, Mabel?" Ralph waited for his wife's answer.

However, Mabel's thoughts were still back with the orphanage near her Virginia home. In spite of all the volunteer hours she spent there every week, the children seldom smiled. "Well, that's a big, powerful machine, all right, but it can't mend a broken heart. It can't make up to a child his or her lost parents."

Ralph curled his arm around his wife, tucking her close to his side. "Maybe not," he said, "but I'll bet this huge machine would bring a smile to their faces, at least the boys' faces. Those kids are lucky you volunteer at the orphanage." He whispered in her ear. "Your love has more power than any machine."

 ## The Master Pattern

You will also know the unlimited greatness of his power as it works with might and strength for us, the believers.

Ephesians 1:19

God has the power to help emotional hurts. Our job is to apply his power, both for ourselves and for others. We can introduce our hurting friends to the same Jesus who performed miracles in the Bible. Talking about the times he has shown his power in our own lives supplies a powerful testimony about God.

Prayer: God, I need your power for the hurtful circumstances in my life. Empower me to help others who are hurting.

Quilt of Valor

"Gramps is coming home." Paige hung up the phone, grabbed her ten-year-old, Carrie, and swung her round and round.

"Yay!" Carrie yelled. "Is he all better?"

"Good enough for the Army to fly him from Kuwait to Walter Reed Hospital in Washington, D.C. That's close enough to see him every week." Paige and Carrie dropped onto the sofa, dizzy from their happy spins.

Brady, Paige's oldest son, came in to investigate all the noise. He perched on the arm of the sofa where his brother Riley climbed onto their mother's lap. "Gramps will have lots of neat stories to tell me about the war," Brady said.

"Like how many bad guys he killed." Riley jumped off his mother's lap, squatting down on his four-year-old legs. He straightened his arm out in front of him and made an arc toward the sofa, aiming his finger. "Pow, pow, pow," Riley fired his verbal "shots."

"Don't expect him to want to talk about the war," Paige warned her children. "Often wounded soldiers don't like to talk about their experiences."

"But Gramps is a hero, isn't he?" Brady asked. "You said he'll get a Purple Heart."

"His heart turned purple?" Riley pounded his chest with his fist. "Neat-o, I'll color my Valentine hearts purple next year."

"His heart didn't turn purple." Brady's voice took on a superior tone. "Purple Heart is the name of the medal he won because he was wounded in the war."

"Pow, right in the leg, huh?"

"That's not funny, Riley. Gramps is in a wheelchair, and I'll bet his leg hurts a lot." Carrie reached out to pinch Riley's leg.

"It did hurt a lot." Paige pulled Riley onto her lap again. "Now he's going to the hospital to learn how to walk on it and get his muscles strong before he comes home. My quilt guild is making him a Quilt of Valor for us to take to the ceremony when he gets his Purple Heart medal."

"I want to help make Gramps a valley quilt," Carrie said.

"Valor quilt, silly," Brady corrected his sister. "V-a-l-o-r. That means brave."

Paige silenced Brady with a look. "We are making a quilt out of red, white, and blue fabrics, using the Bear Claw pattern. We chose the Bear Claw because it seemed like a good symbol for a war hero. Carrie, maybe you could help cut out the little squares for the middle of each set of four claws."

A few months later, the officers presented Grandpa with his medal at the Walter Reed Hospital.

Gramps had progressed enough to stand at attention and say, "For the good old U.S. of A." Afterward, he spread the Quilt of Valor over his legs in the wheelchair.

Six more months passed before he was released from the hospital. The whole family turned out to drive their hero home. They were pleased to see he could leave the wheelchair behind. He even tossed his cane into the car trunk.

"Don't need it," he said, and the family clapped. "Time to play lots of golf." He tickled Riley. "That's what I dreamed about in the hospital." Then Gramps held out his hand. "I'll give you a rest from the drive up here. Give me the keys and I'll drive us all home."

Paige handed over the car keys. "Guess that means you've made a complete recovery."

By the time they reached the interstate, Brady's impatience was rising. "Gramps, you're a traffic hazard driving at ten miles an hour on the interstate."

"Oh, guess I forgot where I am." Gramps looked embarrassed. "In Iraq, I had to drive slow enough to check out the area for roadside bombs."

"You're in the U.S. of A.," Riley piped up, breaking an awkward silence. Everyone laughed at Riley using Gramps's favorite expression for the United States, as Gramps pressed on the gas pedal until he reached interstate speed.

 ## The Master Pattern

They helped David against the band of raiders, for they were all mighty men of valor, and were captains in the army.

1 Chronicles 12:21 NASB

We are all soldiers in the army of God. In every generation, there are raiders who would undermine his kingdom and try to destroy his truths.

Much of the time, the battle is a spiritual one against satanic forces that want to discredit God. But God wants mighty men, women, and children of valor to defend Christianity and the freedom to worship.

Romans 14:17 (KJV) names some of our best weapons to win over people to the love of God. This verse says, "For the kingdom of God is not meat and drink; but righteousness, and peace, and joy in the Holy Ghost." Living uprightly, wearing a peaceful countenance even in times of trial, and living with contagious joy show the power of God to unbelievers.

Prayer: God, use us in our daily lives to demonstrate the character of God to a world which would like to undermine Christianity.

The Burning Bush

"Lindy, what are you up to?" Judy waylaid her poodle before she escaped out the doggy door with her rotary cutter. "Why are you messing in my sewing basket? A plastic fabric cutter is a poor substitute for a doggy bone."

At the word "bone," Lindy sat at Judy's feet, lifted her paw as if to shake hands, and emitted a soft, pleading whine.

"Oh no, you don't. No rewards when you just tried to steal my cutter and lose it who-knows-where outside."

"Mom, I'm missing my pink pj's," Gabby called to her mother down the stairs. "I put them on top of my pillow when I made my bed this morning. I need to pack them for my overnight at Karen's."

"Look in your drawers," Judy called back. "That's where they belong."

"I already looked, and I'm running late. Sarah's dad is picking me up for Karen's party soon."

Judy sighed at the table, where she was quizzing Gary on his spelling words. "Pack another pair," she called toward the stairs. "I'll help look for the pink ones as soon as Gary finishes his homework."

"Judy, where's the sports section of the paper?" Ronald asked his wife from the recliner, where he was sorting through the newspaper.

"How would I know?" she called. "I avoid the sports section at all cost."

"You didn't throw it away did you?"

Ronnie Jr. spoke up: "I took it to look at the scores from the game last night, but I laid it right there on the coffee table. Isn't it there?"

"No," Ronald said. "And I want to read about the golf tournament."

Ronnie Jr. shuffled through the papers with his dad, then resigned himself to watching TV . . . if he could find the remote. "Where is the remote control for the TV?" he hollered. "Don't we always keep it on the coffee table? Did you shove it off, looking for the sports page?" He got down on his hands and knees to look under the table, muttering, "Mom, where's the remote control?"

"Don't ask me," Judy called. "I never have time to watch TV. This family needs a robot or something to keep track of all our things—whoa!" She yelled to Gary, "Grab Lindy! What's she got in her mouth?"

With a lunge, Gary stopped Lindy in her flight toward the doggy door. "It's a dish towel." He pulled it from their poodle's mouth. "You crazy dog. What do you want with that? It doesn't taste good."

An idea dawned on Judy. "She was headed outside with it," she said, tapping the table. "Do you think she's our culprit? Maybe she's taking our things and hiding them outdoors."

"Maybe," Ronnie said. "Hey, I have an idea. Next time we see her headed out with something, let's not stop her. We'll sneak out and follow her. Maybe she'll lead us to some of our missing stuff."

The family didn't have to wait long. Lindy flashed past them within a few minutes carrying a ball of yarn. As soon as she sailed through the doggy door, Judy and Ronnie slipped out too. They watched their poodle head straight to the large Burning Bush outside the garage. The front half of Lindy disappeared under it. Quick digging with her feet sent dirt scattering behind her. She backed up, wagging her tail with satisfaction. When she turned and saw her people, her ears fell, and her tail disappeared between her legs.

Ronnie ran to the bush and lifted the bottom branches. "Lindy, get real! Would you look? Lindy's stashed a bunch of stuff under here. Here's Dad's sports page." Ronnie held up torn strips of crumpled newspaper. "Guess Dad won't read about the golf tourney."

Judy tugged at some pink cloth. "So that's what happened to Gabby's pj's. Yuck, Lindy's chewed on them. It's to the trash can for these. Oh, and here's the remote." Judy handed the control to Ronnie. "But the remote appears full of dirt. Bet it doesn't work anymore."

"Look." Ronnie wiggled further under the bush. "Lindy made herself a bed with our Bear Claw quilt."

"Oh no," Judy lamented. "I wondered why it hasn't been on the sofa the last several weeks." She gave the quilt a shake. "I've got to get this cleaned—it's the last quilt Grandma made before her eyesight failed." Judy shook her finger at the dog. "Lindy, you scallywag. You and your Burning Bush cache. We should have named you Moses, and we probably ought to burn everything you've hidden here . . . but not Grandma's Bear Claw quilt. We'll salvage that."

Judy was the first to return to the family room. "What now?" she exclaimed, since there in the middle of the floor lay one of her prized cosmos plants. A telltale path of dirt gave away how the plant came to rest, root ball and all, across the light blue carpet. A trail of soil and dirt led to the doggy door where several torn branches stuck halfway in and out the door. "What are we going to do with you? Naughty dog. You not only take things out, but you bring in trash too. We never dreamed when we got you, what a nuisance you'd be."

"We never dreamed the doggy door would be a problem either," Ronnie said as he went in search of a piece of wood to board up the escape hatch.

 ## The Master Pattern

There is nothing hidden that will not be revealed.
There is nothing kept secret that will not come
to light.

Luke 8:17

Lindy took objects that attracted her and secreted them in her hideaway. What do we have in our lives we have hidden from the view of our friends or family? What secret habit can't we overcome? Some secret attitudes we don't want discovered but can't seem to root out.

Nothing is a secret from God. He's waiting for us to come to him with whatever we've hidden. He will provide his

Holy Spirit to help us overcome any trial or temptation. We can win over these hidden areas. The power that created the universe is not defeated by our problems. Better to conquer them now than to hear them pronounced at our final judgment.

Prayer: God, help me overcome those attitudes that make me ashamed. Grant me the power of the Holy Spirit to overcome.

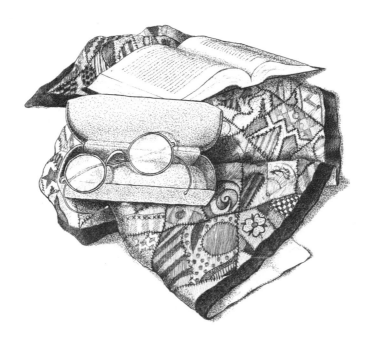

Crazy Quilt

Sometimes made with delicate, fragile fabrics, then embroidered with motifs and sentimental messages, these quilts often represent a different kind of elegance.

Crazy quilts don't provide a warm or practical function as much as an ornamental purpose. Historically, they were often two layers without batting; quilters designed the pieces to avoid right angles to make the design more unpredictable.

Sometimes trimmed with tassels and braid or ribbons and lace, Crazy quilts were symbols of affluence. A person needed spare time to make something decorative instead of practical, and the frequent use of expensive fabrics like velvet or satins in a Crazy quilt also added to the aura of luxury.

Can't Quilt

"It's no use," Abby cried. "I can't make a pretty quilt." She tossed her quilt square onto the coffee table and slunk down on the sofa in her family room. "My Pine Tree pattern looks diseased and deformed."

Kendra laughed. "Maybe piecing little bits of fabric isn't your thing."

"Apparently," Abby said with a sigh. "I guess appliqué isn't either." Abby dug into a drawer in the end table to show Kendra her attempt to appliqué a square with the Love Apple pattern. "These apples look more like trapezoids. What do you think? Maybe I'd be better off using my needles to mount butterflies for your bug collection. Maybe I'll take up bowling instead. Or does dyslexia mess up bowling too? My eyes will see crooked lanes, and the ball will end up in the gutter of the next lane." She crossed her eyes and went through the pantomime of rolling a bowling ball.

"I'll go bowling with you too." Loyal Kendra wouldn't admit defeat. "Why don't you try making a Crazy quilt? Nothing has to be precise. Nothing has to match or look like anything in particular. You can put material together every which way. That's why it's called 'Crazy.'"

"After this disaster, I think I'd be crazy to try." Abby crumpled up her square.

"Come on," Kendra insisted. "Don't resign your needles to mounting bugs yet. I like sewing with you. Let's do a Crazy quilt."

"Well, I have some good material," Abby said. "Mother has all sorts of pretty velvets and silk scraps left over from making bridesmaids dresses for the girls at church." Abby considered the prospect. "Let's give it a whirl. Or should I say a crazy spin?" She went to the corner of the room where her mother kept a trunk of fabric scraps. Abby thought of her neighbor Jody when she moved her Bible to open the trunk. "I wish we could get Jody to come to church with us," she told Kendra. "She got mad the last time I asked her. She said she heard too much God stuff at home. Every time she goofs up, her Dad says she needs a switching to 'make her ready for heaven.'"

"That's awful." Kendra shuddered.

"I told her God loved her, and I told her my Sunday school teacher says the reason we try to improve our behavior is because we love him, not because we're afraid God will punish us. Jody still won't come to Sunday school with me."

Each weekend, Kendra came to Abby's house, and they exchanged teen talk about high school over their quilting. Abby discovered she loved making her Crazy quilt. She sewed different-shaped pieces together and then whacked off an edge, making that piece ready to fit to another at a different angle.

"This is fun," Abby said, seaming an odd-shaped triangle onto a long narrow pink strip.

"Your good color sense makes your quilt look better than mine." Kendra laid her quilt next to Abby's. "I don't mix the color shades as well as you do."

"After the mess I made of my other attempts to quilt, I was afraid to dream this would work out so well," Abby admitted. She added a blue square to a triangle shape.

The high school girls were silent several moments as their Baby Lock sewing machines hummed quietly. "You know what?" Abby said finally. "I think this Crazy quilt has taught me something. Maybe I'm not stupid, like I thought. I thought I couldn't quilt, but I just had to find another way to do this. Maybe with my dyslexia I just need to find a different way to study. You showed me a better quilt pattern for my personality. Maybe someone can show me a better way to learn."

Kendra smiled. "Mrs. Johnson in the counseling office probably can," she said.

For another few minutes the sound of the girls' machines was the only noise in the family room. "Guess what?" Abby said. "You've got me thinking. Maybe we can find a different way to introduce Jody to God's love, since she won't come to Sunday school. In fact, why don't we invite her to make quilts with us? I'll bet she'd like making Crazy quilts as much as I do." Abby held out her work to admire it. "We don't have to talk about God directly. We'll just let Jody know we enjoy her and want to do things with her."

To the girls' delight, Jody turned out to be very handy with a needle, and she soon had each of them embroidering all kinds of teenage sayings on their quilt pieces.

The Master Pattern

Whoever is a believer in Christ is a new creation.
The old way of living has disappeared. A new way
of living has come into existence.

2 Corinthians 5:17

Sometimes we can overcome our difficulties by using a new method or finding a new approach to a situation. In some circumstances, finding the proper approach may require some trial and error. Since every person is different, we need sensitivity to which methods will best reach each person's heart for Christ. Allowing our joy in Jesus to show and loving others makes a good beginning.

Prayer: God, give me the flexibility to try new approaches to difficulties and to show your love to others with joy and compassion.

Lost

Kelly felt happy as she carried her turkey casserole into the church fellowship room. Life was good. She arrived a few minutes ahead of the newcomer class dinner in order to get the coffee ready before the class dismissed. Kelly's quilt hung beside the pulpit. She enjoyed thinking about people looking at the Crazy quilt she'd made. She hoped they found the quilt a pleasant sight while they listened to the history and beliefs of the church they wanted to make their regular place of worship.

As the group filed out for dinner, Kelly slipped into the sanctuary to admire the work she so loved making: the large and elaborate pieces, the embroidered symbols of Christ, adding to the quilt's significance—the lambs decorating some of the patches, roses adorning others; the variety of fish, shepherd crooks, and crosses showing her craftsmanship, the narrow gold cording outlining some of the irregular patches, the gold tassels hanging from each corner.

But Kelly squeaked out a gasp and "What!?" as she entered the sanctuary. The wall where she had hung the quilt was bare. Kelly circled the square room to see if someone

68

had moved the quilt somewhere else. Nothing. She walked down the aisles in case someone had taken it down for some chore and not yet replaced it. Nothing. Her stomach fluttered and her mind scrambled for explanations. By the time she rushed back into the fellowship hall to find her pastor, the flutters had turned to panic.

"Where's the Crazy quilt, Pastor G?" she asked, grabbing his arm.

"On the wall, left of the pulpit," he answered matter-of-factly.

"No," Kelly said. "No, it should be there, but it's not. The wall is blank."

"W-what? It was there this morning when we arrived. It's too heavy for someone to move easily."

"I'm telling you, it isn't there." Kelly grabbed Pastor G's hand and pulled him back to the sanctuary.

Indeed, the wall was bare.

Pastor G rubbed his chin, as puzzled as Kelly. "I'll call the cleaning crew and see if they know anything," he promised.

But the crew didn't know anything. Neither did the pulpit committee or the altar committee. The search widened to include the evangelism committee, the visiting committee, even the garden committee. No one had any idea of the whereabouts of Kelly's labor of love. Announcements appeared in the bulletin. Nothing.

Then the prayer groups prayed.

Finally, people in the congregation began to think the unthinkable: Someone had stolen their beautiful Crazy quilt.

The church secretary called Kelly to offer an idea. "I discovered an internet site that lists lost quilts. Why don't we post a picture and description of the quilt?"

Nothing more to lose, Kelly thought as she posted the information about her lost quilt. She followed up with a prayer: "God, you know exactly where my quilt is." A rush of repentance overwhelmed her. "Oh, dear." She knelt by her chair. "When I gave the quilt to the church, I didn't completely give it to you. I've had so much pride in it, and I've reveled in the praise. If you can use the quilt somewhere else to reach people with the message of Jesus's love, use it that way. If it pleases you to return it, I'll thank you."

She pulled a tissue out of her pocket and continued her conversation with God. "Here I am grieving over my creation, a quilt; but it's merely a thing. If I'm sad over a thing, how much worse it must be to grieve over the people you created because you wanted to fellowship with them, but they won't believe in you and are lost to you."

Mid-prayer, Kelly began to pace the floor. "I don't think I ever had any concept of how much you must hurt over the lost until I lost my quilt," she prayed. "My quilt's trivial, by contrast, to people losing eternal life because they don't accept you."

The extravagance of God's love wrapped around Kelly, warming her heart.

 ## The Master Pattern

Indeed, the Son of Man has come to seek and to save people who are lost.

Luke 19:10

What do you think? Suppose a man has 100 sheep and one of them strays. Won't he leave the 99

sheep in the hills to look for the one that has
strayed?

Matthew 18:12

God longs for everyone to find him. The Bible says God
doesn't want any to be lost. His search is far superior to
any internet scouring of ours. He knows exactly where a
person loses contact with him, and he understands how to
rescue each soul.

Kelly never found her quilt, but she found her mission
in life—to tell people about how much God wants to com-
municate with them. What might you find if you search
your own heart for the things precious to God?

Prayer: God, make me an instrument to reach the lost.

Champ Escapades

"Oh no, you don't." Tiffany chased her miniature bull terrier around the dining room table. She didn't catch up with
him before he reached his escape hatch—the doggy door to
the patio—but the door itself snared him. Try as he might,
Champ couldn't get through the narrow opening carrying
Tiffany's metal ruler in his mouth.

"Drop it!" Tiffany put all the authority she could muster
into the command.

In a rare act of submission, probably born from his failure
to get the ruler through the door, Champ flopped down at
her feet and spit out the ruler he had snatched from her
quilt bag.

"Good boy." Thinking it a good idea to award obedi-
ence, Tiffany scratched her mischievous dog behind his
ears. "What am I going to do with you? I should call you
Chomp instead of Champ, since you fill your days with
chewing everything in sight."

Champ whined as if to apologize and laid his head on her shoe.

Tiffany picked up her terrier and settled him onto the sofa beside her. She pulled her Crazy quilt onto her lap and began to embroider the last of the buttonhole stitches around the irregular quilt pieces.

She flipped on the TV, intending to listen to her favorite game show while she worked. Instead of the program she anticipated, a man was preaching. She didn't want to wake up Champ, who finally had fallen asleep on top of the remote control, so she listened while the preacher talked. He was telling about Gideon and a companion who dreamed of a barley loaf falling into the Midian camp.

Tiffany thought how she had never dreamed a dream worthy of attaching such spiritual significance, and she smiled at her stitches. *My dreams seem more haphazard than this Crazy quilt I'm making,* she thought.

She didn't know how long she worked before an ominous gagging sound made her look around. Champ wasn't beside her. She threw down her quilt and headed for the sound. There on the kitchen counter Champ sat licking the remnants of a pan of brownies from his mouth.

"You didn't eat the whole pan of brownies, did you?" The empty pan gave silent evidence that he had. "No, no, Champ. You are too small to eat that much—and chocolate! Dogs aren't supposed to eat chocolate. Now I'll have to give you ipecac, or those brownies will poison you for sure." She turned to the cabinet and took out the ipecac bottle. Maybe Champ recognized the bottle from previous episodes of gluttony or maybe his chocolate binge made him feel sick. In either case, a race was on as he jumped off the counter. His legs whirling like a cartoon animal, Champ dashed into the family room and up on the sofa with Tiffany close behind. Those ominous sounds began again, and Champ spewed his overindulgence all over the nearly finished Crazy quilt.

"No! Champ!" Tiffany shrieked. "Look what you did!" Champ was too sick to even shrink away as she grabbed him. He managed one more heave on the quilt before she picked him up and ran outdoors with him, stroking his belly and carrying the now-soiled quilt.

"Velvets and silk notwithstanding, this quilt top is going into the washing machine," Tiffany pronounced. She hosed off the mess. Then she marched the dripping quilt top into the house and dumped it into the washer. She set the machine on gentle, hoping the unfinished edges wouldn't fray very much, and turned the knob to "start."

In the meantime, Champ, recovered from his chocolate binge, pushed through his doggy door and sat at his doggy dish wiggling his backside.

"No you don't," Tiffany said. "No more anything for you." Champ licked her leg. "Where's your self-discipline?" she chastised the terrier. "The very idea of eating a whole pan of brownies." *And just what did you do with the pint of ice cream at lunch?* The thought grabbed Tiffany like a collar as she thought of her own excesses. She laughed at herself and stooped over to look Champ in the eye. "Okay, okay, buddy. We both have trouble knowing when to stop eating, but I still say you are the champion rascal. I don't dream about loaves of bread like Gideon. I dream about ice cream. Do dogs dream about chocolate?"

74

The Master Pattern

When you find honey, eat only as much as you need.

Otherwise, you will have too much and vomit.

Proverbs 25:16

Good-tasting food challenges one's self-discipline. But when taste buds tempt us to overindulge, we can pray for self-discipline in the area of our appetites, whether they be for food, drink, or overstimulating movies and television. Modcration benefits both body and soul.

Prayer: God, help me exert self-discipline and avoid all areas of excess. Impart your power to me that I may resist temptation.

Embellish

I've never seen such an amazing quilt, Olivia thought, stopping near a Crazy quilt richly encrusted with beads of all colors, shapes, and sizes. The woman in front of her backed up, bumping into Olivia. For a moment, Olivia's nose was buried in the lady's orange coat. Olivia drew back. *What was that strange odor from the coat?*

She waited for the crowd around the quilt to move so she could get a closer look while staying far enough from the orange coat to avoid its different odor.

"May we see the back?" asked another woman, wearing astonishingly low-hung pants, revealing a roly-poly bare midriff.

The white-gloved museum docent obligingly lifted one corner of the quilt so spectators could see the back. "The artist quilted the random designs made by the beads, instead of following the edges of the Crazy quilt fabric pieces," the docent noted. "I like the different approach."

You would. Olivia looked at the docent's mix-matched plaid, flowered, and striped outfit.

Maggie, who created the quilt, stepped up. She was wearing the orange coat and odd, heavy perfume. "I had a lot of fun embellishing this quilt. I let out all the stops."

"You really did." Olivia moved forward. "I've never seen anything so rich in beading. This quilt looks fit for the parlor of a queen. What a gorgeous effect!" She resisted touching the beautiful piece. Instead, she backed up, overpowered by the strong scent of Maggie's perfume.

"I named it Bead Stew," Maggie said. "I dumped into one container all the beads left from many different projects—makes for a faster cleanup than trying to sort them back into each tiny bottle, especially those itty bitty beads. I mix them up, and when it's time to embellish something, I just reach into the bowl and sew on whatever comes out first. I keep on taking them out in random order. It's fun to see the effect. Pretty nice, don't you think?"

Olivia agreed. The beads sparkled in the overhead light. The varied jewel tones of the fabric pieces enhanced the different effect of the beads on each patch. Olivia couldn't help but eye the other spectators, standing around her admiring the quilt, too. Some wore chic, elegant clothes. Some were dressed for comfort. A few wore outfits which defied fashion. Others even carried distinctive odors like the orange coat and the artist's perfume. But they were all equally entranced with the beadwork.

Olivia found herself wondering how the group admiring the prize-winning quilt would look, if an overhead camera took a picture of them. Individually they might appear just as random in size, appearance, and style as the beading on the quilt. *Did God take as much joy in his design of people on the earth as the artist took in her unpredictable placing of beads? Was each one's idea of what to wear, what style to enjoy, even what smelled good a source of delight to the Creator of the universe?*

Olivia regretted her silent criticism of her fellow festival attenders. Together, they all had a part in some unknown, not understood pattern of God.

The world, she thought, really is God's People Stew.

 ## The Master Pattern

You are Christ's body and each of you is an individual part of it.

1 Corinthians 12:27

There are different ways of serving, and yet the same Lord is served.

1 Corinthians 12:5

There is room in God's world for all kinds of people. Each one of us is designed by God to fulfill a particular place and role. Rather than judge and criticize one another, we do well to ask God to help us view each other as his glorious creation and search for the extraordinary pattern he wants to build using the cooperation of people.

Prayer: God, give me tolerance for the people you created. Help me to see them through your eyes. Create a lovely design with your people.

School House

Quilters often chose red fabrics to use in the School House pattern, though sometimes each house was done in different fabrics and colors.

Since education was valued by the early settlers of America, the school was often the first public building built in new communities as the settlers moved West. Pioneers simply copied the school from their previous home when they settled into their new location, so schoolhouses often looked the same. Sometimes this pattern is adapted to look more like a private home. Frequently, sashing strips separate the schoolhouse squares and provide a unifying effect.

Quilted Comfort

"Bummer, bummer, bummer!" Emma turned over and pulled the hospital sheet over her head. On the opposite wall, the television announced the time and location of all the local high school graduations.

"Agreed." Her mother, Sheila, punched the remote to silence the news. "Big time bummer." Sheila leaned over the hospital bed and patted her daughter's shoulder. She had run out of words of comfort.

"Why did I have to get sick before my graduation?" Emma sat up and flung her arms around her mother's neck.

Sheila dried both of their tears with the sheet.

A brisk knock and excited chatter interrupted the woebegone moment. A group of Emma's classmates marched into the room, wearing blue mortarboards, carrying a large gift-wrapped bundle, and filling the room with noise and motion.

"Since you can't come to graduation, we brought some of graduation to you," Kate, a dear friend, said. She put a blue mortarboard on Emma's head.

"Here's the program." Alice propped it on the bedside table. "Your name's in it."

"And here's our gift." Rachel handed a bundle to Emma. "Open it."

Emma squealed when she opened the package. "A wall hanging!" She spread it over the bed. "Red and blue schoolhouses. How did you find a quilt with our school colors?"

"We didn't find it," Kate said. "We made it."

"I didn't know you knew how to quilt," Emma said. "You've been holding out on me."

"Read what we embroidered." Kate turned a corner over to show the quilt label on the back.

Emma read: "In honor of Emma Grant upon her graduation from Valleyville High School, June 19, 1975." She blinked and clenched her jaw to hold back more tears.

"We all embroidered our names on the schoolhouses." Rachel pointed to her name.

"How did you do all this work on such short notice? I've only been in the hospital two days."

"That's why it's only a small quilted hanging," Kate said. "That, and all our moms helped us, or we wouldn't have finished it."

"It's perfect. I can hang this size anywhere."

"Ready for 'Pomp and Circumstance'?" Rachel pulled out her harmonica and played the traditional graduation procession tune. The five girls surrounded Emma's bed and marched in place while they hummed the famous tune.

Emma slipped out of bed and tugged her intravenous pole until she was lined up with the girls.

"I pronounce you an honor graduate of Valleyville High." Sheila switched Emma's tassel on her mortarboard from one side to the other, and the other girls changed theirs too.

Kate took her camera out of her pocket. "Do the tassel thing again. I want to take pictures."

"We brought cupcakes too," Rachel said. The girls set out a plate of cupcakes iced in blue with a red "V" for Valleyville on each one. Sheila borrowed Kate's camera and flashed pictures while the girls ate.

Kate checked her watch. "We've got to go because we have to line up ahead of time for the procession in the stadium," she said. "But we want to leave you with this inspirational book for graduates. We hope it will help you look at the bright side."

"Read what the principal wrote to you inside the cover," Rachel prodded.

Emma's voice faltered as she read: "Your outstanding accomplishments in high school make us proud. Your record is more important than attending the graduation ceremony. The ceremony is not as significant as the skills and knowledge you developed and the maturity you gained. Character lasts, ceremonies fade."

With hugs all around, Emma's friends left her in much better spirits.

"This wasn't exactly the way I dreamed my high school graduation ceremony would go," she told her mother when the room was quiet again. "But it was better than I thought it would be an hour ago."

"You have A-plus friends." Mom smiled.

The Master Pattern

The seeds that were planted on good ground are people who also hear the word. But they keep it in their good and honest hearts and produce what is good despite what life may bring.

Luke 8:15

Everyone's plate of life holds some helpings of disappointment. How we handle those dashed hopes, broken promises, and unexpected setbacks will test our character. We don't always pass the test as well as we would like. That's when the body of Christ, the support of fellow believers, sustains us. By demonstrating love and acceptance toward one another during times of trial, we help bring out the best in ourselves and our friends.

Prayer: Help me find creative ways to offer my friends support and comfort in their times of disappointment.

Fabric Bartering

"Good day, Widow Rainville. Don't tell me you weren't going to ask me what I need from your store." Dr. Baylor strode from the window display to the counter in the general store.

"Oh, Dr. Baylor, I'm sorry I didn't recognize you." Mildred Rainville squinted.

"That's not like you," he said. "Why, I could have stolen these hammers in the window display as easy as pie." Dr. Baylor motioned toward the display of tools. "How's your eyesight, Mrs. Rainville? Is it time for me to make you stronger glasses?"

"I'm sorry, Dr. Baylor, I would come to see you about glasses, but I just don't have the money to pay you." Mildred shoved her glasses up on her nose.

"These are hard times, all right. This war between the states has milked us North Carolinians dry." Dr. Baylor's tone was sympathitic. "But it won't do to go without your eyesight. You need good vision to keep up the store and add up the figures every day. We don't want anyone cheating you."

"Not many customers these days. Folks are barely eking by, and no one has much to spend." Mildred pointed to her cash register. "Only a few coins today."

"Tell you what," the good doctor said. "Let's arrange a barter. I'll check your vision and make you some stronger glasses and you give me one of these lovely bolts of calico and throw in a sack of flour." The optometrist picked up a bolt that had tiny blue flowers sprinkled over a red background. "My missus has been wanting to make a School House quilt. She thinks if we raffle a quilt with schoolhouses on it, we'll make enough to pay for the salary of the teacher of these youngsters around here for at least one term. War or no war, we don't want our children growing up not knowing how to read or write."

"Is one bolt really worth a pair of glasses?" Mildred didn't wait for an answer. "That's a right good idea. I've got a lot of extra time between customers, what with the war taking every cent. With my new glasses, I'll make a quilt myself and barter it to old Mr. Siler at the dairy. If I can buy milk, cheese, and flour to sell in the store, more people might bring something into the store that they can trade for food staples."

"I would, for one," Dr. Baylor said. "Making glasses takes enough time that the wife and I barely manage to keep up with our vegetable garden. If we all cooperate together, we'll survive these frightening days. Tense times call for cooperation."

Dr. Baylor's idea caught on in town.

Before long, Mildred had bartered most of her fabric bolts for other goods. With blockades off the southern coasts, she couldn't restock. But her neighbors weren't defeated. They made quilts from their curtains and sent them to the front where the Confederate soldiers were fighting. Mildred's little store became a center for quilting bees where lively talk provided a welcome distraction from worry and busy fingers brought the women the satisfaction of helping.

The economy didn't blossom in Widow Rainville and Dr. Baylor's small North Carolina town, but folks developed skills at making do. The people grew close enough to one another that they felt free to discuss their dreams for the future, and the women offered one another comfort when the news was bad and rejoicing when it was good.

 ## The Master Pattern

> The one who received ten thousand dollars brought the additional ten thousand. He said, "Sir, you gave me ten thousand dollars. I've doubled the amount." His master replied, "Good job! You're a good and faithful servant! You proved that you could be trusted with a small amount. I will put you in charge of a large amount."
>
> Matthew 25:20–21

During the Civil War, the people in the South suffered from many shortages but their ingenuity enabled them to survive.

God still supplies ingenuity for whatever life brings us. He gives us abilities to earn money, and we are responsible to use our abilities diligently. We also carry the responsibility of spending our money wisely. God entrusts our income to us.

The King James Version of this passage uses the word "talents" to mean money. In addition to the meaning of money, we know that God does plant many varied talents and skills in each one of us. Using those talents brings fulfillment and satisfaction to us. Since our money, talents, and skills are all gifts from him, we seek his guidance on how to use them; he gives us the opportunity to demonstrate our faithfulness in small ways before he entrusts us with larger responsibilities, gifts, and blessings.

Prayer: O Lord, help us use our money wisely. Show us how to use our talents to bless people and expand your kingdom.

Pockets

"Can I sleep in the bed with the Pocket Ladies?" Kim carried her overnight bag into her grandmother's house. Her mother greeted Grandma Smithers and gave her daughter a goodbye hug.

"Be a good girl. I'll pick you up Sunday night after Daddy's business convention is over. It's only a short trip."

"Don't worry." Kim smiled. "I won't be lonely with the Pocket Ladies to talk to."

"Who are the Pocket Ladies?" Grandma Smithers asked, waving to her daughter as she drove out of the driveway.

"You know," Kim said. "Those ladies with the very big skirts sewn on your quilt. The ladies must be schoolteachers because they live between the schoolhouses on your quilt. They probably need the hankies in their pockets to blow the noses of the children in the schoolhouses."

Grandma Smithers laughed. "My, my, you have the most charming imagination. Let's get you settled in your room."

She took Kim's bag, and they climbed the stairs. "Is this the room where you want to sleep?"

"Yes." Kim jumped onto the bed. "Hi, Pocket Ladies." Kim took a lace-trimmed, organdy hanky from the blue gingham pocket of one of the wide-skirted girls on the quilt. She rubbed her nose with it. "See, it's too small for a real girl, but it must be the right size for the children who go to the schoolhouse." She rubbed the hankie over the red schoolhouse in the next quilt square.

Grandma laughed. "When I made that quilt, I had no idea what fun it would be for my granddaughter someday."

Kim was more than willing to take naps on her bed at Grandma's. To entertain herself while Grandma rested, she unpacked her comic books and read them out loud to the children in the schoolhouses, which lay between each billowing-skirted schoolmarm.

Sunday, Mom and Dad arrived to pick up their six-year-old.

"Just a minute," Grandma called cheerily when Kim answered the door and swooped onto the porch, greeting her parents with a hug. "I'll be right down and I'm bringing your overnight bag."

However, Grandma's face was less cheerful when she stepped onto the landing with the suitcase in her hand. "Kim," she asked, "What has happened to the hankies from the quilt on your bed? They're all gone, not a single hanky left in any of the pockets."

"I'll bet they were too tempting." Mother frowned. "Kim, did you lose them?"

"No," Kim looked at the ground. "They're right here." She opened her suitcase and pulled a handful of lace-trimmed white organdy from it. "They're dirty 'cause they wiped the noses of so many children in all the quilt schoolhouses. I need to take them home and wash them."

Mom, Dad, and Grandma Smithers stood still, processing Kim's earnest words.

"But weren't you sort of stealing them?" Dad finally spoke.

"Oh, no. I'm going to wash them and bring them back."

"But they belong to Grandma." Dad knelt down beside his daughter.

"Kim, you must not take things that belong to someone else without permission. Grandma's quilt wouldn't be the same without the hankies in the pockets."

"I just wanted to play washing at my house." Kim's lip began to quiver.

Grandma Smithers put her arm around Kim. "Well, now, I do believe Kim knows the difference between stealing something that doesn't belong to her and trying to do a favor with something she likes at lot." Grandma looked up at Kim's parents. "I have some coffee ready for your mother and father. How about you wash out the hankies in the kitchen sink and dry them on the back porch while your parents tell me all about their trip? Then you can help me put the hankies back in the pockets on the quilt, and they will be ready for you to play with the next time you come. The hankies wouldn't be nearly as much fun to wash at your house without the ladies' pockets to tuck them into when they're dry."

Kim smiled. "When I sleep under the School House quilt with the Pocket Ladies, I dream of being a schoolteacher," she announced, then skipped into the kitchen to begin her laundry.

The Master Pattern

Your laws make me happy. I never forget your word.

Psalm 119:16

The enemy of our soul knows just how to package something to make it tempting. Having God's word established in our lives protects us from mistakes that would otherwise result in unhappiness.

While Kim's young mind probably didn't intend dishonesty or stealing with her hanky-washing scenario, she did need to learn more about how to prevent her actions from being misinterpreted and how it was important to show respect for someone else's property. Her Grandma chose not to see her actions as wrong, and she understood the universal joy of delighting the heart of a grandchild.

The Lord also knows what delights our hearts. Creating happiness in our lives brings God a greater joy than we can comprehend.

Prayer: Ground me in your laws, O God, that I might find happiness. Make my heart a vessel that brings you joy.

Quilt Me a Hug

Jeannie's mood didn't match that of her lunch companion. Tracy exuded energy and excitement even when ordering mundane grilled cheese and coffee. Jeannie duplicated Tracy's order, the easiest way to handle the numbness that filled her soul.

"How long can you give me this afternoon?" Tracy asked once the waitress left.

"Lunch won't take long, if you're in a hurry," Jeannie replied. "How long does it take to eat a grilled cheese sandwich?"

"Well," Tracy baited, "I have a great plan for us if you have time."

"Me? I'm living in a state of suspended animation since Dan died. It's hard to summon enthusiasm for anything."

"Look what I brought." Tracy spread out a group of photos on the table.

"That's Dan on our last campout." Jeannie picked up the snapshot.

"And this one is of the two of you by Ruby Waterfalls."

"A good picture, even if my tongue was hanging out from the climb." Jeannie sounded more animated.

Tracy smiled. "Look at this one."

Jeannie's eyes widened. "How'd you get a picture from our honeymoon?"

Tracy smiled even wider. "My little secret. Here's the picture of Dan turning his pockets inside-out after your daughter's wedding."

Jeannie laughed.

"Listen to my wonderful idea." Tracy scooped up the pictures to make room for the lunch plates that arrived.

"After we eat, let's go to Cheryl's Quilt Shop at Miller's Corner and transfer the pictures to fabric."

"Wouldn't a scrapbook be the best place for these pictures?" Jeannie mused.

"Sally sells vest patterns," Tracy explained. "We'll alternate fabric with Dan's picture on it and some other quilt square pattern of your choosing to make you a vest. When you wear it, you'll be wearing a hug from Dan."

Jeannie's mouth dropped open. "That's the best idea I've heard in a long time—and I even know which pattern to use between the pictures, the School House pattern. After all, Dan taught school for twenty-four years before becoming the principal of his school."

Each morning the thought of Tracy's project nudged Jeannie out of bed. Working with the pictures of her husband gave her pleasant memories of their years together, and the memories were a comfort.

"You came up with the best prescription for depression and grief of any I've tried," Jeannie told Tracy after she finished the vest. "You're right. When I wear or even hold this vest, I do feel as if I'm in a hug from the love of my life."

She told her friend how the project was healing in even more ways too. "When I began sewing again," Jeannie said, "I realized I had also stopped my morning Bible time. I began reading Scripture and talking to Jesus before I began stitching; at first, I struggled. All I could think about was *why—if God's so powerful, why did he let my Dan die?* I told God my true feelings and then I'd look at the pictures on my vest, and I'd think how many blessings God gave us. It took weeks, but as I appliquéd the schoolhouses, happy memories of Dan's school began to push aside my resentment. I felt a renewed love for God."

Jeannie spun around to show off her vest as Tracy clapped.

"Now I think I can start doing more than going through the motions of living," Jeannie said. "I think I'll start volunteering at the Christian high school where Dan was the principal. I can be an example to the staff about how important it is to keep communicating with Jesus, especially when life seems to fall apart. I like the story of the woman who touched Jesus's garment and was healed. We need to touch each others' lives when someone is having trouble touching Jesus. You did that for me." Jeannie hugged her friend. "We can be the warm hug that makes a person able to touch Jesus again."

 ## The Master Pattern

Whenever he would go into villages, cities, or farms, people would put their sick in the marketplaces. They begged him to let them touch the edge of his clothes. Everyone who touched his clothes was made well.

Mark 6:56

Busyness, disappointment, grief all conspire to keep us distanced from Jesus. The time we feel the most despair is the time we most need to reach out to touch God. Sometimes we need the help of a tangible object such as our Bible or a friend to make the connection back into the loving hug of God. He's always ready to touch our lives. As we follow Jesus, we are able to help others back to God. He'll meet even the slightest move in his direction.

Prayer: God, help me touch you with the innermost parts of my heart so that I can overcome the tangles of my life that would pull me away from you. Help me draw close daily. Give me the ability to draw other troubled hearts close to you.

Drunkard's Path

With its concave-curved pieces, this quilt requires skill because attaching the quarter-curved edges is a challenge and the pattern depends on combining blocks in order to achieve the overall design.

The Women's Christian Temperance Union sometimes made these quilts for fund-raising and raffled them at state fair booths. Many Temperance Union quilts used blue- and white-colored fabrics, since those were the colors for the organization that sought to protect the home from the ravages of alcohol.

Sometimes this pattern was called Indiana Puzzle.

Blown Around

"I see you're up to your eyeballs in a new project," Linda said when she stopped in to bring Emma her order of co-op food.

"Come see the quilt I'm making," Emma said. She led Linda into the dining room where blue and white curving pieces covered her entire dining table.

"What a pretty blue," Linda said, fingering one piece. "This looks like a complicated pattern. What's it called?"

"Drunkard's Path." Emma laid another piece in its proper sequence.

Linda tipped her head sideways to survey the fabric lay-out. "Maybe that's an appropriate name. It does have a bit of a dizzying effect with all the curves and turns."

"That's why I lay every piece in place before pinning or sewing," Emma agreed. "The pattern is complicated to arrange properly. I don't want to make a mistake and alternate the blocks in the wrong direction. It's easy to get one or two of the pieces backward and mess up the overall effect."

"It looks perfect to me."

"My kids tease me. They say I'll need to hide it when Uncle Jeb comes since he gets drunk enough without the help of a Drunkard's Path quilt." Emma's laugh carried a rueful note.

"I didn't know you had a brother with an alcohol problem."

"It's not the kind of thing one brags about. My kids may laugh, but Jeb's alcoholism is no joking matter. My brother's life is messed up. His kids are embarrassed by him and once in a while they report being afraid of him. It makes my heart ache." Emma turned into the kitchen. "Let's make some tea. I'll tell you the latest chapter in the saga of poor Uncle Jeb. Don't worry. I'll not bore you with all the bygone history. Only rarely does he get mean when he drinks. Most of the time, he gets silly and does foolish things. He's been passed over for promotions again and again because his attitude seems irresponsible when he's drunk." Emma filled her teakettle and set it on the burner to heat. "My parents are heartbroken over their son. We weren't exactly a picture-perfect family, but they had better dreams for the future of their firstborn."

While Emma poured boiling water over tea leaves, she was surprised to hear her husband, Harry, drive into the carport. She looked out the window and wondered aloud, "Now why would Harry be home early?"

"Hi, honey, I'm home," Harry called, stepping into the kitchen. "Wait 'til I tell you about the latest mess at work." He stopped when he saw Linda and heard the teakettle whistle.

"Ah, tea for two friends. Do you have enough for me?" Harry pulled a cup from the cabinet. "You'll never believe what my boss did today. John lost his temper and conducted a shouting match with the president of our largest contractor. Talk about lack of self-control! Was our vice president hot!" Harry loosened his tie. "I wish I had the nerve to talk to John about his temper, but after today's explosion, I can see he's not the type to listen to advice. He could sure use a seminar straight from Proverbs."

"Is that why you came home early?" Emma poured tea for all three of them.

"Yeah, most of us faded away and left the poor vice president to try to smooth things over with our top contractor. The man's face was red hot. Speaking of hot, it's hot in here. What's the thermostat set on? Let's get more ventilation."

Harry stood in the doorway of the dining room and flipped a switch.

Emma screamed, "Nooo!" But she was too late.

Harry stood still in shocked dismay at the result of his innocent action. The breeze from the overhead fan blew all two hundred of Emma's carefully arranged quilt pieces off the table onto the floor.

"I'm so sorry," Harry whispered. "I didn't know."

 ## The Master Pattern

God's word is living and active. It's sharper than any two-edged sword and cuts as deep as the place where soul and spirit meet, the place where joints and marrow meet. God's word judges a person's thoughts and intentions. No creature can hide from God. Everything is uncovered and exposed for him to see. We must answer to him.

Hebrews 4:12–13

> Jesus said to them, "Aren't you mistaken be-
> cause you don't know the Scriptures or God's
> power?"
>
> Mark 12:24

Sometimes our plans are blown apart because of innocent or annoying mistakes. Other times our mistakes carry serious consequences. Either way, God cares and wants to help us.

We are vulnerable to erroneous actions or decisions when we don't know what God's word says. Jeb relied on alcohol when he really needed the power of God. Harry's boss didn't know God's power was available to help him curb his temper.

When we are well versed in what the Bible says, we understand that God cares about our messes, whether of big or small importance. We can call upon his power to guide and help us in our everyday living.

Prayer: God, we ask for your help in discerning how to apply Scriptures to our everyday life. We call upon your power to help us live godly and productive lives according to your will and ways.

Learning and Stitching

"Did you hear about the latest trial in the Stone's household?" Belinda didn't look up from the needle she rocked at a fast pace through the quilt stretched over her quilting bee frame.

"What now?" Lori asked. "That household has had one tragedy after another."

"All the children have measles." Belinda's needle stopped. "Sybil fears little Stewart's eyes are affected. He might even lose the sight in his right eye. She's wrapped a scarf around his eyes to keep out any light."

"Poor Sybil and Reb. First their daughter Wanda ran off with the traveling medicine man, then grasshoppers destroyed their entire corn crop. The bank is still threatening to take their house. Now this." Lori shook her head.

"I told her she shouldn't let her children run around outdoors when it's raining." Tabitha shook her finger in the air. "If she'd listened to me, Stewart wouldn't have measles."

Belinda tried to restrain herself from glaring at Tabitha. "People have to do their chores for their cattle, rain or no rain," she said.

"How does Sybil stand all those troubles?" thirteen-year-old Dolores asked, feeling grown up, quilting with the ladies.

Dolores's little sister, Myrtle, stopped picking up threads and pins under the quilt frame as she listened to the women. She often played with Stewart. "Will I get measles too and go blind?" she wondered.

"Don't worry, child." Lori patted Myrtle on the head. "We'll pray for protection from the disease."

"Your children shouldn't be listening to adult conversation," Tabitha scolded Belinda.

"They learn a lot about how to handle life at these quilting bees," Belinda defended herself. "Sybil is a good example for them. Sybil says heartaches and trials are part of life. Her exact words were, 'Into each life comes some rain, and this must be my rainy season.'"

Dolores forgot to stitch as she listened.

"Sybil also said, 'It's not what happens to you so much as what you do with what happens to you.' I'm glad for my daughters to learn from the values you women demonstrate."

Dolores felt like it was a dream come true for Mother to allow her to join the women's quilting bee. They were stitching a Drunkard's Path quilt to give their pastor in celebration of his tenth year at their little church. Wanting to sound grown up, she spoke: "Won't the pastor think it's strange to give him a quilt called the Drunkard's Path? Won't he think we are criticizing him or something? He preaches against drunkenness at least once a month."

Her mother answered, "When I asked his wife, she said the pattern is perfect. He can hang it in his office as a handy visual aid when he counsels people about alcohol problems. He can remind them that liquor causes twisted paths."

"Poor Sybil." Tabitha clucked her tongue. "You couldn't blame her if she turned to drink."

"She doesn't need drink," Belinda replied. "Drowning her problems would only provide a temporary solution. She turns to Jesus instead. She asked us to pray, so when we break for lunch, let's remember to pray for God to touch Stewart's eyes."

Dolores looked from her mother to each of the women. She was silent in her own thoughts.

"Stitch, dear." Belinda nudged her daughter with her elbow.

Dolores shook off her thoughts, and poked her needle through the layers.

After lunch, the women rose to leave. Belinda put a lid on the kettle of leftover chicken soup and handed it to Tabitha. "Do me a favor and take this home to your family. Mine have eaten it too many meals in a row. Here, hold down the lid with the leftover biscuits." Belinda wrapped a flour sack towel around the biscuits and set them on top of the kettle lid. "Dolores, help Tabitha carry her things to her carriage."

"Why didn't you send the soup to the Stones?" Dolores asked when she returned to the house. "Why did you give it to that sourpuss Tabitha?"

Belinda smiled gently. "The sour one probably needs love the most."

Dolores hugged her mother. "When I get married and have girls, I'll include my daughters in my quilting bees too. I learned more than stitches."

"Quilting bees offer a real slice of life. A realistic view helps us keep our dreams of what life should be like in balance," Belinda said.

 ## The Master Pattern

Open your ears, and hear the words of wise people, and set your mind on the knowledge I give you.

Proverbs 22:17

Don't refrain from discussing the difficult parts of life with children. Expose them to many wise people when they are young. Even adults profit from observing how wise people react when things go wrong. When we see how people in difficulties trust God anyway, it strengthens our faith. Watching wise people helps us sort out the trivial from the important. When we gain God's perspective we can more easily dismiss the less important.

Prayer: God, teach us to see things through your eyes. Give us your values and the ability to cope with difficult situations. Help us, in our thinking, to minimize rather than inflate our problems.

Hide the Quilts

Tilly urged her horse to run faster. Once home, she ran up the front steps, but fell over a board that had loosened and fallen from the eaves of the porch overhang. Still, Tilly wasted no time. "Ma! Come quick," she called. "A telegram!"

Maude Gordon hastened to answer the alarm in her daughter's voice. She stooped to help up Tilly, who winced as she stepped down on her ankle.

"Ma," Tilly cried, "the Rebels defeated the Union forces only a few miles away. They're marching right now through Kentucky, toward us."

Eyes wide with alarm, Ma helped Tilly limp to the porch swing. "The telegram said soldiers are stealing animals, food, and blankets."

Maude Gordon rang the dinner bell for her boys. "I was afraid it would come to this. Our most treasured possession is Grandma's prize-winning Drunkard's Path quilt. We can't allow the Rebels to steal it. We'll hide it."

"Where?" Tilly tipped her head back against the swing cushion and elevated her ankle. "The telegram said the soldiers ransacked the houses." She looked around. "How about there?" She pointed above her head to the space in the eaves over the porch that the fallen board revealed.

James and John hurried in from their wood cutting.

"The Rebels are coming," Ma announced, then directed James to bring Grandma's Drunkard's Path quilt from the blanket chest. "We'll tuck it into the eaves and whatever else we can fit in there. John, get some nails and a hammer to put back this board once we've finished our stash."

Ma and James stood on chairs and stuffed several quilts in the eaves. Then they gathered up jars of canned beans and peaches and tucked them into the space too, before John nailed back the board.

"Hope the Rebels won't look there," John said, surveying the fast handiwork.

Ma bound a strip of long sheet around Tilly's swelling ankle, as John spotted a cloud of dust on the horizon.

"How could a marching column get here that fast?" James said.

"Maybe they're scouts going before the main army."

"Everyone find a chore and look busy," Maude told her children.

James grabbed a hoe and began to work on the weeds in the flowers around the front porch. He piled the weeds on top of a basket of eggs to hide them. Through a slit, Tilly stuffed her pillow with onions and then lay back on the cushion. Maude tucked small bags of cornmeal under Tilly's skirt, then covered Tilly with a blanket. She left Tilly's bandaged ankle exposed and elevated on another pillow. Next Maude snatched up a broom to vigorously sweep the porch.

An officer in Confederate gray drew his horse to a stop. A dozen men pulled up beside him. "Ma'am," the captain said, lifting his hat to Maude. "We need food and supplies."

"We don't give anything to enemy. . . ." Jamie began with a defiant look. Maude allowed her broom to slip from her hand and to whack Jamie in the head before he could finish his sentence.

"Oh, sorry, Jamie. I lost control of the broom." She glared at him,

"We'll just look around for what we need. We won't harm anyone, as long as you all stay right here. Winter is coming on, and we need lots of blankets." The captain sauntered into the living room as if he'd been invited.

"This will make a fine cover." A soldier reached for the blanket over Tilly.

But Tilly held it tightly. "Can't you see I'm hurt?"

The soldier poked at her ankle. "Hmm. It's swollen. How'd you sprain it?"

"Ow!" Tilly let tears flow when he poked again.

The captain returned to the porch. "Leave the poor girl alone." He motioned. "She's hurt."

Tilly shivered, thinking this day seemed a nightmare.

Men who had fanned out over the house returned with blankets, a large sack of flour, and one of sugar. Another tooted on Pa's clarinet.

Jamie grabbed for it. The soldier laughed and jumped off the porch.

The Gordons watched silently as the captain picked up another quilt still on the porch railing and tossed it to a soldier on the nearest horse. "Something fine to sleep on," he said.

Not as fine as you would have found, if we hadn't hid Grandma's quilts, Maude thought. She resisted the urge to look up at the porch eaves, but Jamie stared overhead.

"Thank you, ma'am," the captain said.

Ma's hand over Jamie's mouth muffled his response.

The Master Pattern

I am in trouble, so do not hide your face from me. Answer me quickly!

Psalm 69:17

We are never hidden from God. He knows about even our small troubles and always sees the complexities of our situations. God never hides from us. He hears our pleas for answers and helps us find solutions to our problems.

Prayer: God, hear our cries when we are in trouble. Show us your answers. Hide us from our enemies.

Comparing Quilts

The people admiring the quilt hanging next to Tara's crowded out the view of her quilt. Tara changed her position, moving to the other side of her quilt, but second thoughts nagged her. *Maybe standing by my own quilt at a quilt show isn't such a good idea*, she wondered.

"Hi, Tara. I found you." Cora gave her friend a hug.

"I'm so glad to see you. No one has taken the slightest . . ." Tara's words trailed off when her friend turned her attention to the large elephant on the next quilt.

Interest in my quilt, Tara finished, silently, to herself. The Drunkard's Path quilt Tara made hadn't won a prize, not so much as an honorable mention, but she knew the work was good that she had put into it, and she wished someone would take just the teeniest minute to see it.

"Wow, your quilt is like a picture book history lesson." Cora was talking to the lady who made the unusual piece next to Tara's quilt. A large elephant dominated the design with one big, gray, three-dimensional ear. "Did a New England man really invent a machine that cut elephant tusks into thin slices for piano keys?"

"Sure did. He made lots of money."

"Reading what you have written and pictured here, I don't think many Americans in that day understood the suffering that ivory caused African natives." Cora grimaced. "I didn't know their own people made them carry heavy loads of ivory from inland African to the coast for shipping to this country. Your quilt makes it clear they suffered pain, even death, getting ivory transported to ships for America."

Cora read every word written on the amazing quilt and joined in the chorus of praise for the details that pictured the sad story behind ivory products.

"You've done a good thing, educating us about a portion of history we didn't know," Cora told the exhibitor. "Knowledge keeps us from repeating the mistakes of history, right, Tara?" Cora turned to her friend.

"Right," Tara agreed.

"I'll finish the rounds to see the other quilts," Cora said. "Want to meet me at the restaurant across the street for dinner?"

"Sure."

Cora was off, leaving Tara standing by her quilt. *She didn't even glance at my work.* Tara swallowed her disappointment.

The creator of the spectacular quilt was called away, but her elephant pattern continued to attract viewers. Tara remembered all the amazing stories the quilter told about her creation so she, too, began to tell the spectators, helping them enjoy every aspect of the unusual piece. Cora was right. The quilt presented an important history lesson, one that everyone needed to know to ensure that such thoughtless cruelty never happened again.

When she had arrived at the show that morning, Tara expected to feel joy because her lovingly constructed Drunkard's Path actually hung in a quilt show. Instead, she began to enjoy sharing the story of another woman's project when people stopped to see and hear the story of elephant tusks.

Just before closing, Cora dashed up to Tara. "I said I'd meet you at the restaurant," she said, "but I was so carried away by this quilt." Cora gestured toward the elephant creation. "I never even saw your quilt." Cora stood back for a good look. "Tara, it is lovely. The label says it's called Drunkard's Path. Did you make it for a gift?"

"Yes, for my sister. We're very close and I wanted to show her how happy I am about her success with Alcoholics Anonymous. She just celebrated ten years of sobriety."

"She'll be speechless with delight," Cora said.

With that remark Tara was able to let go of her goal for her quilt. She realized she hadn't made it for praise. She had made it for love.

 ## The Master Pattern

> Anger is cruel, and fury is overwhelming, but who can survive jealousy?
>
> Proverbs 27:4

Jealousy, a destructive emotion, can sneak into our thinking without our recognizing it. How important, though, to recognize when jealousy tempts us.

The consequences of jealousy are even more grave than those for anger or fury. When we recognize jealousy in our soul, we must take steps to root it out. Tara overcame her jealousy by recognizing a better motive for attending the quilt festival. She helped people enjoy the object of her envy.

For us, prayer is a help, and like Tara we can then turn our thoughts and energies to finding the good in whatever arouses our jealousy.

Prayer: God, help me recognize when jealousy seeps into my thinking. Help me find ways to root it out and find good that counteracts jealousy.

Tumbling Blocks

The optical illusion of a three-dimensional block on this pattern comes from the careful arrangement of colors cut in diamond shapes. The pleasing effect may not have been planned originally, but perhaps resulted from a chance arrangement of fabric and then was copied, growing in popularity in the New England region.

For the Tumbling Block design, pieces of dark, medium, and light colors are always carefully arranged in the same direction, then pieced together, taking care where the corners come together to create the illusion. By using light or shiny material to represent the tops of the blocks, the three-dimensional effect is created. Polished cotton is often chosen to create the smooth, light-reflecting effect of the blocks. This illusive pattern is found as far back as the eleventh century in Italian tile floors.

Fabric Stealth

"I'll never buy fabric in here again." Adrian snatched her package off the counter and rushed out of the store before angry tears betrayed the extent of her hurt.

Nora followed her, more than a little embarrassed and disturbed by the altercation she witnessed between her friend and the discount store saleswoman.

"Once I bought the material, it belongs to me, and how I use it in my quilt is not the store's business." Adrian's heels pounded the parking lot as she hurried along. "What I do with the material is my choice—and I made a good choice or my Tumbling Block quilt would not have been allowed as a juried entry in the contest for our town's quilt show."

Nora moved aside to stay out of the way of the bag of fabric that Adrian swung about in anger.

Adrian kept fuming: "The very idea of that clerk criticizing my fabric choice. These are the same colors I used for my juried entry because I'm going to make another one for a gift." Tears won over her anger by the time she reached her car, slung her package of red polished cotton and matching calicos onto the backseat, and shoved the key into the ignition.

Nora ran to catch up and scrambled into the passenger seat. "I thought buying a couple of yards of that red chintz had the same effect on the saleswoman as it would on a bull in a bullpen," she said. "I didn't think she would let you buy it. She was rude."

"It's none of her business how I use my material." Adrian continued to sputter her resentment and thrust the car into gear.

As Adrian sped out of the lot, Nora kicked off her shoes. She rubbed one foot. "Warn me when our itinerary includes racing across a parking lot to escape enraged saleswomen. I'll wear tennis shoes."

"Wear them tomorrow," Adrian said. "We'll walk our toes to nubs at the quilt show. I'll pick you up early so we can get in before the crowds. I'm hoping my quilt wins an honorable mention, at least."

The next morning, halfway down the first aisle, Adrian's excited anticipation morphed into horror. Her beautiful Tumbling Block quilt hung in a prominent place, but instead of sporting an award, the wide red chintz border was discolored all along the bottom. Orange cones warning "wet floor" bracketed the quilt. Yellow crime tape stretched between them and held back a growing crowd. A docent squatted behind the tape, mopping liquid from the floor.

"I'm so sorry." The president of Adrian's quilt guild hurried over to her. "I wouldn't have believed it, if I hadn't seen it myself. Just minutes ago, right after opening, a woman ran in here and threw bleach on your quilt. Another lady identified her as a salesperson at the discount store. Police are going there now."

A crowd gathered around. The onlookers all talked at once.

"I hope they charge her with vandalism."

A tall lady agreed. "I'd be furious, if that was my quilt."

Another patted Adrian's shoulder. "Think of all your hard work only to see it ruined."

"You'll have bad dreams about this for months."

"Why would that storekeeper be so mad at you?"

Stunned, Adrian's mind struggled to process all the angry things people said.

Nora's voice finally penetrated the babble of outrage and declarations of vengeance. "You bought matching chintz yesterday. I'll appliqué it over the damaged part. If you look closely you'll see the damage is restricted to the wide border. Don't worry, we can fix it." Nora put her arm around her friend.

"Yes, we'll fix it." Adrian straightened her shoulders. She looked around her at the quilters expressing their distress at the vandalism and raised her voice to be heard. "The police and the courts will take care of the woman who damaged my quilt. I'm going to work at forgiving her."

 ## The Master Pattern

Don't take revenge, dear friends. Instead, let God's anger take care of it. After all, Scripture says, "I alone have the right to take revenge. I will pay back, says the Lord."

Romans 12:19

When someone wrongs us, our anger urges us to get even. Wisdom requires us to take the situation to God, trusting him to do what is right. We don't want to get in the way of God's plan, which is much wider and deeper than we can comprehend.

Prayer: Lord, help me forgive instead of seeking vengeance. Help me to trust you to take care of offensive, hurtful situations.

Stitching the Hard Way

"Grandpa, could you turn on the generator?" Ada found her grandfather on the porch reading his newspaper by the waning evening light.

"Can't waste the gas it takes." Grandpa turned a page without looking up.

"But you turn it on when you need light to whittle at night."

"Whittled pieces sell to the tourists and customers at our vegetable stand, and my whittling buys you shoes, missy. It's enough of a favor that we're raising you." Grandpa lifted his head in time to see Ada's stricken look. "Why do you need electricity?"

"I'm learning to sew on Grandma's electric sewing machine. You turn the generator on when Grandma wants to sew." Ada tried to filter out the whine creeping into her voice.

"Not when she *wants* to sew, when she *needs* to sew. That's different. Needs as in she needs to make your clothes when you outgrow the old ones. She needs to make me shirts, and she needs to hem new sheets for our beds. What do you need to sew?"

Ada thought the word "need" sounded sarcastic when Grandpa used it. But she had her answer ready. "I need to make a baby quilt for my Sunday school teacher. She's going to have a baby after the first of the year."

"Show me you can sew something worth the time and money, and I'll see about turning on the generator for you someday." Grandpa pulled the paper up close, intent on finishing it before evening fell and it became too dark to read.

"Okay, Grandpa. I'll show you. I'm going to make a Tumbling Block quilt for Mrs. Taylor. You'll see, Tumbling Block quilts are pretty. Don't worry," she added before he could protest. "I'll just use scraps from Grandma's sewing. You wait and see how warm Mrs. Taylor's baby is next winter, wrapped in my quilt." She stopped herself from saying he was stingy.

Ada watched her grandmother when she sewed the next shirt for Grandpa. Grandma turned the little wheel on the right of the machine with her hand, while she gently pressed the knee bar on the machine until the motor reached just the right speed for sewing. Then she took her hand off the little wheel. With both hands free, she guided the material under the needle. Her knee on the bar kept the electric machine purring.

Ada decided that if her grandpa wouldn't turn on the generator, she would turn the little wheel with her right hand and sew. Ada had helped Grandma cut out diamonds to make a Tumbling Block quilt before. They even had some pieces left from the project.

First, she cut out more pieces, enough to make a small baby blanket. Then she pinned the diamond pieces together; with her left hand, she guided the diamonds under the needle while she rotated the wheel with her right hand. With great persistence, considering her slow pace, she kept turning the wheel over and over until she sewed the diamonds together into blocks. Then she began the same process to sew the blocks together. Finally, she decided she had it big enough for a blanket, even if it wasn't as big as the ones Grandma made for babies.

"A baby's very tiny when it's first born," Ada said, rubbing her arm. "I think a baby quilt can be quite small, and turning that wheel takes so long."

Grandma nodded.

When the quilt was finished, Ada wrapped it in leftover paper Grandpa used when he wrapped his whittled pieces. The next Sunday she took the blanket to Mrs. Taylor.

When Mrs. Taylor opened the gift after Sunday school, Ada waited anxiously.

"Is it too small?" she asked, her eyes anxious.

"It's the perfect size," Mrs. Taylor said, hugging Ada. "How did you make such a lovely quilt?"

"The electricity wasn't on so I turned the wheel on Grandma's machine by hand."

"Oh, my." Mrs. Taylor then seemed speechless. She laid the little quilt over her lap and reached out to plant a kiss on Ada's forehead. "No one ever had a better-sized quilt to wrap around a newborn. This is perfect for bringing our new baby home from the hospital."

"Could you tell Grandpa I sewed something worthwhile?" Ada's eyes searched Mrs. Taylor's face.

The Master Pattern

Dear Children, you belong to God. So you have
won the victory over these people, because the
one who is in you is greater than the one who
is in the world.

1 John 4:4

Victory doesn't always come easily. Sometimes we must
struggle and persist in the face of obstacles. If we ask, God
will grant us the motivation to keep at it. There is no problem God cannot conquer. For our part, we pray for his guidance and persist, and it is God who does the overcoming.

*Prayer: God, make us willing to persist to achieve the goals
we believe you have for us. Give us the patience to find the
paths we can use even when the way is hard.*

Cut It Right

Donna grabbed her blue tote and joined her daughter and granddaughter on the deck of their beach cottage. *Three adult generations are stretched out on these lounge chairs,* she thought, smiling. "We just need the umbrella for shade," she said.

Her granddaughter Hannah jumped up. "I'll get it," Hannah said.

Donna frowned. "I don't think you should be carrying the umbrella in your condition."

"Not to worry," Hannah said, laughing. "I don't even show yet. Anyway, the umbrella's light."

"I don't want any harm to come to the baby." Grandma patted Hannah as she set up the umbrella on the picnic table.

"Nancy, I have a favor to ask." Grandma Donna addressed her daughter, "You're the expert quilter. Years ago I began a Tumbling Block quilt. I made a good-sized piece for the top, and then put it aside. Later I made another good-sized piece with the same fabrics. My plan was to put them together to form one quilt." Grandma Donna made a wry face. "The problem is I didn't check the size of the blocks on the first half before I cut the second half." She opened the blue bag and spread the two halves of the quilt onto the table.

"See," she said. "I cut the pieces in the second half slightly larger. Now the two pieces don't fit properly side by side." Grandma demonstrated. "I want to give Hannah's baby a quilt, but I don't see well enough to make another one." She turned to Nancy. "I want you to make these two pieces into a quilt. You have seven months to do it."

Nancy shut her eyes against the sun—and her mother's proposition.

"Beautiful, Grandma." Hannah clapped her hands. "I love the Tumbling Block pattern for baby quilts."

Nancy swallowed the word "impossible" before it tumbled from her lips.

"See how they look funny together," Grandma looked again at the pieces set side by side.

Nancy did indeed see how funny they looked. *Impossible,* she wanted to say but didn't.

"I should have checked the dimensions before I cut out the second set of pieces." Grandma shook her head.

"Mother can figure out something," Hannah said, smiling.

Sure, Nancy thought, *and I can jump over the moon and make my cat play the fiddle too.* She studied the pieces with her chin in her hand.

"When do you want this finished again? By the time the child starts school?" Nancy couldn't contain the sarcasm.

"No, no." Grandma didn't smile. "When the baby is born. That's seven months isn't it?"

"Yes." Hannah beamed approval. "Isn't it exciting the baby almost has its first quilt?"

"Almost," Nancy repeated. *Maybe never.* She gathered up the pieces and put them back in the blue bag. "I'll take it home. We don't want to get the fabric all sandy down here at the beach." *I'll think about it later—if ever*, she thought, zipping up the blue bag.

Vacation or not, those two pieces of quilt haunted Nancy's dreams at the beach. She found herself searching for a solution as she turned from side to side, night after night.

Seven months later, she plopped a package on her daughter's bed in the maternity ward. Hannah opened it, and both she and Grandma exclaimed over Nancy's eye-pleasing quilt solution while their tiny fourth generation slept in her mother's arms, unaware of any efforts made on her behalf.

Nancy had cut the finished panels in half, turned the two with the smaller tumbling blocks diagonally and sewed them together as a center panel. She sewed the larger block pieces on each side, and attached a border around the whole thing to even it. The design was lovely and looked as if it had been planned that way from the start. Both Hannah and Grandma clapped.

Nancy pointed her finger toward the ceiling. "God helped me."

"When I wrap your grandbaby in her beautiful quilt, I'll bet her dreams will be beautiful too." Hannah kissed the newborn's forehead.

 ## The Master Pattern

My dear brothers and sisters, don't be fooled. Every good present and every perfect gift comes from above, from the Father who made the sun, moon, and stars. The Father doesn't change like the shifting shadows produced by the sun and the moon.

James 1:16–17

Whether we've sinned or merely goofed up, God is ready to help us find his solutions. Our responsibility is to ask for his help, and then give him the credit for solving our problems.

Prayer: Thank you, Lord, for the gift of solutions. Thank you that you have answers for every situation, even those that are seemingly inconsequential. Reveal your solutions to me.

Straight Stitching

"Come in—the door's not locked." Madison's listless voice barely carried to her friends, who knocked on her apartment door.

"The cheer-up committee is here," Emily announced, poking her head around the door. "May we come in?"

"Sure. But I warn you I'm not an easy patient to cheer." In spite of her words, Madison used her good right arm to push herself upright on the sofa. She managed a smile to greet her friends as they entered.

Emily, Joyce, and Candice each hugged their friend, careful to avoid the IV in Madison's left arm.

"If you'd like, you can heat some water for tea in the kitchen." Madison gestured toward the doorway. "Sorry to ask you to wait on yourselves, but this is one of my IV hooked-up hours, and I get tired of dragging this IV pole around."

"A friend in need is a friend indeed, or something like that," Candice said, disappearing into the kitchen to the groan of her listeners.

"You can count on Candice for a cliché," Emily said. "We brought you a present." She put a bulky brown paper package on the sofa.

"Well, sort of a half-present," Joyce said, smiling.

"Wait, I'll get the kettle going before you open it," Candice called over the sound of running water from the kitchen. "Polly put the kettle on, and we'll all have hot water," she sang.

Madison grinned. "I've missed Candice's sayings."

"Are the intravenous meds conquering the infection in your elbow?" Emily asked.

"The blood work shows some improvement, but the infection is still there. I'm so sick of lying around week after week feeling useless."

"Useless no more. We brought you a project."

"What kind of project can a one-armed bandit do?" Madison lifted her left arm, showing its limited movement.

"Where's your will? We brought the way." Candice came in with her usual contribution of mix and match sayings.

"If I think too much, I get scared it's never going to heal," Madison confessed. "Dr. Moss says the only recourse in that case is surgery to remove the elbow." Her eyes teared up as her friends gasped.

"No." Emily stamped her foot. "Not with the cheer-up team praying for you."

"We'll banish that kind of thinking with our cheer-up project," Joyce said. "Here, open our package."

Emily helped Madison pull off the brown paper.

"A Tumbling Block quilt." Madison's eyes sparkled with delight instead of tears. "It's beautiful and it's . . . not finished." Madison turned a questioning look at her friends.

"We want you to quilt it," Emily said.

"And just how will I do that with one arm?"

"Here's the system," Joyce explained. "You hold the needle steady in your left hand and thread it with your right. Then, you hold the quilt hoop still with your left hand while you stitch with your much more mobile right hand. We made the tumbling block pattern because all your stitching will be along straight lines. Emily, show her how it works."

Emily took charge. "First, position the quilt. Next, stitch the straight line, reposition the hoop, and repeat. See? Simple." Emily positioned the quilt under Madison's left arm, then demonstrated how she could turn it for the next line of stitching in another direction. "We thought curves would require more repositioning, hence the tumbling block pattern."

Madison tried. "It works," she said, surprised. "Here I've felt useless and couldn't even enjoy my favorite hobby. Thanks." She reached out her right hand to pat each friend in turn. "I always think pleasant thoughts when I quilt. It seems like the best time for thinking about life and God's plans. Our lives are kind of like a quilt in his hands, aren't they? It's a good time to consider all God's blessings. Maybe that's why I find quilting so relaxing."

"Maybe relaxing thoughts will do you more good than medicine," Joyce suggested.

"Your cheer-up committee has come to banish fear," Emily said, waving an imaginary wand over Madison.

Candice accompanied her with an off-key rendition of a song from *Cinderella*: "A dream is a wish the heart makes . . ."

When her friends groaned, Candice asked, "Isn't there a saying about how one woman with a dream can trample down an empire?"

"Candice!" Her friends, even Madison, called her name in unison and rolled their eyes.

 ## The Master Pattern

A man that hath friends must shew himself friendly: and there is a friend that sticketh closer than a brother.

Proverbs 18:24 KJV

Jesus is our friend who sticks by us through thick or thin, as Candice would say. He inspires us to demonstrate our friendship with one another and meet needs in creative ways. When we lay our friends before God in prayer, he will help us find ways to bless one another and deepen our friendships beyond our imagination.

Prayer: Lord, help us encourage and comfort one another. Give us insights into how to deepen our friendships.

Le Moyne Star

This pattern was named for Pierre Le Moyne, a French explorer, soldier, and statesman. In 1699, his family was given a grant of land known as Louisiana, and Pierre is credited with establishing New Orleans in 1718.

The quilt named for him contains an eight-pointed star pattern. Each part of the star is a diamond-shaped piece, and these diamonds repeat in matching or contrasting colors throughout the quilt. Occasionally, the quilt consists of one large eight-pointed star, with shaded sections instead of smaller stars. In English-speaking territories, the name of the quilt became Lemon Star.

Matching

Frances picked up a tattered cardboard carton and hesitated. "I hate to put this box in the attic. We've nearly worn it out, carting it all over the United States each time the Navy moved us these last twenty years."

"What's in the box?" Grace was helping her new neighbor, Frances, settle into the base housing next to her own. "Maybe you should give it to Navy Relief, if you are tired of moving it with you." Grace took the box from Frances and set it by the door with the other items that Frances had decided wouldn't fit well in her new quarters.

"I can't do that." Frances picked up the box again. "It's a quilt my mother started more than twenty years ago. She couldn't finish it because arthritis crippled her hands too much for sewing. I promised to finish it for her."

Grace frowned slightly. "After all this time, would she care if you didn't?"

"Probably not," Frances admitted, "but I care. I want to honor her by finishing the project. Mother said the stars on this Le Moyne quilt represented her dreams. She had already finished the star squares and sewn about half of the green sashes between them. I think, somehow, not finishing the quilt disappointed her and contributed to a despairing attitude toward life. It might brighten her attitude, if I finished it now." Frances peeled back the loose tape and opened the lid.

"Oh, yes, do it now," Grace said, leaning over to see the pretty multicolored star patches in the box.

"Oh, but maybe I've waited too long." Frances pulled out different pieces of fabric. "There's not enough green material to finish the sashes between the squares. Some of the biggest and best fabric stores in the nation were located in the city where we lived last. I had no idea there were so many shades of green. I don't think there's any way now to match this particular green." She sighed, "I guess I procrastinated too long."

Grace's eyes twinkled. "Maybe not. You'll never guess what I do as a hobby." She gripped Frances's arm. "I create dye shades and hand-dyed fabrics." Grace held up a square with its green strips sewn around it. "We can match this. I'll show you how."

Frances stared at her. "You can do that?"

"The beauty of hand-dying is that all the subtle variations in a piece of fabric look intentional. Even if we don't get a complete match, we can create shades that will blend well."

"Do you have time to help me with this old project?"

"I'd love to." Grace took the liberty of lifting the squares and sashes out of the carton. She exclaimed with excitement over the lovely stars made from a variety of printed material.

"I'll take a piece of this fabric home with me," she told Frances. "Come over as soon as you get your boxes unloaded. I'll show you how I dye material. You're right, there are a lot of subtle differences in the shades of green, but we can match this."

Frances took Grace's offer for help, and was thrilled with the result. "I wish I'd met you before this," Frances told Grace. "My mother could have been enjoying her quilt instead of spiraling into despair. I think she became hopeless to begin with, and even angry at God, because she had to stop her favorite activity, which was quilting. Maybe this project will help her make peace with God. She thinks God can't use her because of the anger she's held against him. She's closed the door to his love because she's spent so many years mad at him."

"Nonsense," Grace said. "If I can dye a plain old piece of muslin and make it blend nicely with another piece, surely God can make her life blend nicely with his plans for her."

"What a good thing to tell my mother," Frances said. "I'll say those very words when I give her the finished quilt."

 ## The Master Pattern

I know the plans that I have for you, declared the LORD. They are plans for peace and not disaster, plans to give you a future filled with hope.

Jeremiah 29:11

God's thoughts toward us are full of love even when we aren't matching up to his desires for our lives. When we turn back to God, he is ready to restore us, to match us up to his plan, to make us fit into the lovely pattern he began in us when he created us.

Prayer: Lord, help us put away resentment when things disappoint us. Restore our love for you and use us in your kingdom.

Sew Lonely

Todd breezed in the door and threw his hat on a peg. "Want to go with me tomorrow?" he asked his wife. "I'm going to town to buy some hardware for mending the barn door latches. I'm going to drive the wagon because I want to lay in supplies for other jobs I can do when winter arrives." He slipped behind his wife, who stood at their wood stove, and wrapped his arms around her waist. "I'll bet I'll have enough money left over to buy something that would tickle your fancy, and we'll have that long ride to talk." He nuzzled the back of Lannie's neck.

Lannie turned around to tip her face up for Todd's kiss. "We won't have anyone *but* each other to talk to come winter," she said. "I'm still not used to these frozen winters here in northern Minnesota. No use thinking about socializing when the winter storms begin. Even our nearest neighbors are too far away to risk coming over without an important reason."

"Today I peeled and canned all the ripe tomatoes," Lannie said. "Yesterday I canned the cherries from the tree." She waved her wooden spoon toward a row of glass jars, cheering the room with their red provision. "I've even tried my hand at making sauerkraut like your mother. Our stomachs won't growl this winter, but my soul will."

Todd tried his best to think of ways to alleviate his wife's loneliness on their farm close to the Canadian border. He knew Lannie was far away from her big family of sisters back in Maryland. "Maybe you'd fancy buying a book while we're in town," he suggested. "We could read to each other when winter isolates us."

Todd cuddled her closer. "The last newspaper I read reviewed Gene Stratton-Porter's new book, *A Girl of the Limberlost*. A book is good for our minds."

"Sounds interesting. I'd love to go to the mercantile with you and chat with Nelly Windle. This time I think I'd fancy buying thread and batting and some bright-colored calico. When Minnesota weather pins me inside this house, I can create a beautiful quilt instead of losing my mind."

"We'll take turns then," Todd said. "I'll read to you while you quilt, and you can read to me while I whittle some utensils. We'll make a blazing fire and be as snug as two kittens in a patch of sunlight." Todd pressed Lannie's head against his shoulder. "I wish I could be enough for you, but I guess women need other womenfolk."

Lannie nodded her head, feeling the comfort of his tweed jacket rubbing against her cheek. "I love you, Todd, and reading *A Girl of the Limberlost* together sounds like fun. It's just that up here, there are so many months when it's so cold you'd freeze your tongue to the pump if you tried to get a drink of water. The skies stay gray, and the world closes in on me." She ran a finger down his cheek. "But I agree that your reading while I make a colorful Le Moyne Star quilt will be a good distraction and keep my mind busy."

Todd daydreamed for a moment. "I hear that the telephone people are running lines way out into the country," he said. "One of my dreams is that by this time next winter, our wheat crop will yield enough that we can afford to sign up for a telephone party line. Then you can visit with the women in town, even when snow drifts keep us on the farm."

Lannie beamed. "Nelly has a party line where she lives in town, and she learns lots about her little community just by listening."

"I'll bet." Todd winked and stepped away to peek under the lid of the kettle on the wood stove. He laughed heartily. "When we get the phone, you better stick to talking about quilt patterns and colors so the whole village won't know our business."

 ## The Master Pattern

Call to me, and I will answer you. I will tell you great and mysterious things that you do not know.

Jeremiah 33:3

We never receive a busy signal when we call out to God. Regardless of how lonely we are, how isolated our circumstances, how distressed we feel, God always hears us when we pray. We can speak honestly with him about our feelings and needs. He delights in our communication with him and he will, indeed, show us the miracle of his love.

Prayer: God, help me remember to call on you when I'm lonely. Help me make you my first call when I'm in distress. Draw me close so that I learn to hear your comfort and grow in my communication with you.

Durable Patterns

"Ready, Miss Daugherty?" the orderly asked, rolling the stretcher into her hospital room.

"Just a minute." Gina held up her index finger, then picked up a little pair of scissors and hunched over the Le Moyne Star quilt she had spread over her lap. She snipped a few stitches to release the point on one arm of her eight-pointed star. "I guess I'm ready," she said, standing and folding up the quilt in progress. "I'll just have to restitch that last point later," she said to herself. She turned to the orderly. "I hope the doctor does a better job of cutting and stitching my gall bladder than I did with my Le Moyne Star." Her attempt at a laugh sounded nervous.

"Is that the name of your quilt?" the orderly asked, tucking the sheet around her after he helped her onto the gurney. "I didn't see anything wrong with those stars. They looked pretty to me."

"My cardboard pattern wore down as I drew all those pointy pieces, and the last ones didn't have as sharp a point as the early pieces," Gina explained. "I think I'll make a new pattern before I cut out the rest of the star points."

Glad for the distraction the orderly's conversation offered, Gina chattered on about her quilt. *Anything,* she thought, *to keep from thinking about my surgery.* Then: *If merely getting my gall bladder removed dissolves me into a mass of quivering nerves, is my dream of becoming a nurse's assistant reasonable?*

"Next year in my nursing program, I'll be assigned to work on the floor," she told the orderly. "Do you like your job here?" The gurney she rested upon rattled down the hall.

"Sure do," the orderly said. "I have a reputation for calming patients as I take them to surgery. Maybe you can work on this floor." The big man continued to talk about the benefits of his career until they reached the operating room.

Gina sat up on the gurney to see her surroundings better. Complex equipment, blinking lights, bleeping machines. "Looks complicated," she thought aloud. "I wonder if I can learn enough to work here someday."

"Sure you can." The orderly smiled.

Gina turned her head to stare at the large x-ray mounted over lights. It showed her gall bladder, the duct to her pancreas, and her small intestine. She gulped as the anesthesiologist approached.

"I'm leaving you in good hands, Mrs. Daugherty." The orderly gestured toward the surgeon who stood studying the x-ray. "Doc," the orderly said, "is a fine craftsman." To Gina, he said, "You'll have more trouble finding Doc's stitches after you heal than the ones on your quilt."

The next thing Gina heard was the sound of laughter. When she managed to open her eyelids, heavy with sleep-inducing drugs, her surgeon was smiling down at her.

"The operation went fine, Mrs. Daugherty." His smile grew wider. "Tell me, what would you want with your x-ray?"

"X-ray?" Gina's mouth felt dry. A nurse slipped a straw in her mouth so Gina could sip some water.

"You've been asking to take home your x-ray ever since you started to come out of the anesthesia. Never had a patient ask for an x-ray for a souvenir before."

Gina felt a blush heat her cheeks. "I remember. Just before the medicine put me to sleep, I was thinking my x-ray was made from a good stiff material and would make durable patterns that won't wear out when I cut lots of quilt pieces from it."

The doctor laughed, took down the x-ray, and laid it on her chest. "There's a first time for everything," he said. "Happy quilting."

 ## The Master Pattern

The earth and the heavens will disappear, but my words will never disappear.

Luke 21:33

God's Word will last forever. Our bodies aren't so durable, but our spirit is. God gave us the Bible to guide and comfort us all our days on earth. The power of his Word will never disappear. Even more exciting, he wants us to spend eternity in his presence. When our earthly body wears out, we will bask in his glorious presence in heaven because we believe that Jesus Christ took our place on the cross and our sins are forgiven.

Prayer: Thank you for the gift of the Bible, God. Help me to read it faithfully and give me revelation from its words.

Fabric Choosey

"You'll never guess what I've decided to do." Carla swung her purse onto a table and sat down next to her husband on the sofa, cradling a shopping bag on her lap.

"You decided to go shopping," Logan said. "I don't need three guesses to win." He peered into the bag. "What did you buy?"

"It's not what I bought, but what I'm going to do. I'm going to make a quilt."

"Do you know how to make a quilt?"

"I will after I read this wonderful pattern I bought." Carla pulled out the directions. "It's called Le Moyne Star. Isn't it pretty?"

Logan raised his brows in question. "It looks complicated. Don't you need to take a class or something if you want to begin a new hobby?"

"A class would take too much time," Carla said. "Look at all the pretty material I bought. Don't you just love how all the blue prints blend together?"

"How much?" Logan picked up a length of blue corduroy. "Looks pretty expensive to me."

"You won't care how much the cloth cost, when you snuggle with me under this warm quilt on a cold night." She held up a thick piece of batting. "The thicker, the warmer, I decided. Nothing but the best for our quilt."

Later, however, even Carla began to consider Logan's question of "how much" as she proceeded with her project. Her fingers began to hurt from the pressure of her scissors after hours and hours of cutting lots of diamonds for the stars. Her stylish-printed corduroy was tough to cut.

She went back to the store. Dixie sold her a rotary cutter to cut with instead.

When she reached the step of sewing the diamonds together into stars, it didn't take her long to realize corduroy was too thick to make neat sharp points like the ones shown on the pattern. Another trip to the store and Dixie, the clerk, helped her replace the expensive corduroy with more manageable cotton prints.

Her final frustration surfaced when she began to quilt after sandwiching her thick batting between the top and the back layers. Her choice of the thickest batting made it hard to push through the short little needle. She took her project back to the store for advice.

"You just missed a wonderful class on making quilts with stars," Dixie told her as she looked at Carla's quilt and immediately saw the problem. "Oh my! Quilting that batting with those needles won't be easy."

"That's why I'm here," Carla said with a groan. "I need advice."

"You could quilt it on a sewing machine, if you use a heavy-duty needle," Dixie suggested.

"But my dream has always been to hand make a quilt. It seems so much more old-fashioned and traditional, don't you think?" Carla looked pleadingly at Dixie.

"Well, there's a way you can handquilt it if you buy a frame, but you can't just rock the needle in and out of the fabric with such thick batting. You'll need to push the needle all the way through with one hand on top, grab it underneath, and position it to push through to the top with the other hand." Dixie demonstrated the technique.

"Oh bother," Carla said. She sighed. "I should have asked your advice before I began."

"We have a class on machine quilting."

Carla brightened. "Sign me up," she said. "I'm not going to waste all the time and money I put into this top and not do a good job quilting it, dream or no dream. Logan told me I needed to take a class in the first place."

 ## The Master Pattern

Listen to advice and accept discipline so that you
may be wise the rest of your life.

Proverbs 19:20

Life is full of choices. Some are insignificant and some affect our entire lives. We use wisdom when we ask people who are respected in their fields of endeavor for counsel.

Developing a pattern of checking our choices against the wisdom of others protects us from making decisions that waste our time and resources. Seeking wise counsel helps us keep our priorities straight. The most important decision we make in life is what priority we will give to God:

"Choose today whom you will serve . . . my family and I will still serve the Lord" (Joshua 24:15).

Like Joshua, we have many values competing for our allegiance in today's society. The world offers so many attractive ways to spend our lives. But like Joshua, we will prosper when we put God first.

Prayer: God, help me not become distracted by attractive busyness. Help me stand firm in the choice to put you first in my life.

Love Apple

Because the appliqué process takes time, people reasoned that women who made appliqué quilts had the luxury of leisure time, and owning an appliqué quilt made a statement of affluence and prestige.

The Love Apple motif took its design from the tomato plant, which was considered poisonous in the early days of our country and grown in the flower garden as an ornament rather than for food.

This pattern became popular in the mid-nineteenth century, with a design that represented a ripe tomato cut in half and always made from some shade of red materials. Often the section in the center was a yellow print to represent the seeds; the effect was of a fruit people thought stimulated love.

Mismatched

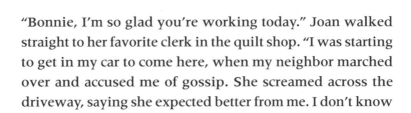

"Bonnie, I'm so glad you're working today." Joan walked straight to her favorite clerk in the quilt shop. "I was starting to get in my car to come here, when my neighbor marched over and accused me of gossip. She screamed across the driveway, saying she expected better from me. I don't know what to do."

Tears started down Joan's face. "I guess my neighbor was right," Joan said in a quavering voice. "My church circle did talk about the baby my neighbor put up for adoption before she was married, but I didn't say a word." Joan clutched a bulging white pillowcase.

"You were silent while others talked?" Bonnie raised her eyebrow.

"I know. I was wrong. I didn't *stop* the gossip." Joan's face felt hot. "I listened. I should have interrupted and said, 'Her past is past and let's not talk about it,' but I kept putting it off because I was afraid to sound preachy." Joan grimaced, reflecting on how she had failed her neighbor. She plopped her pillowcase on the counter. "Guess that makes this quilting problem sound trivial. I'm embarrassed to admit my inertia and procrastination also created this problem."

Bonnie chuckled. "Can't be worse than confessing you let your neighbor down. Don't worry. I think I've seen just about every mistake possible to make on a quilt. I've seen nearly every solution too. Try me."

Joan shook out her quilt top from the pillowcase onto the counter.

"There's one thing you've done right," Bonnie said. "You're storing your quilt in cloth, instead of a plastic bag. I can't tell you how many deteriorating quilts we see because they were stored in plastic—the fast track to discoloration and dry rot."

Joan unfolded her quilt top.

"Why it's lovely," Bonnie said. "After that build up I didn't expect you to show me such a pretty piece. You've appliqued a beautiful Love Apple quilt, so what's the problem?"

Joan sighed. "I thought the Love Apple pattern was the perfect design to use as a wedding present for my sister and her fiancée twenty-two years ago. But I let one thing or another keep me from finishing it. After a while, my sister's marriage began to disintegrate. Watching the deterioration of that relationship was like watching an apple rot."

"Oh," Bonnie said sadly.

"My sister finally divorced several years ago," Joan said, "and I put the unfinished quilt away. Since her daughter is marrying this year, I thought I'd finish the quilt for my niece instead . . . but I can't match the gold material I used for the border."

Joan set two gold material strips on the counter. "My original intention was to create a quilt large enough for a double bed, but my niece is going to have a queen-size bed. I thought I'd add another gold border, but look at these fabrics side by side. The new and the old don't match."

Bonnie studied the pieces and thought about the pattern. "What about putting a thin strip of red material between the gold stripes?" she suggested. "The red color would carry the color of the apple from the center into the border and separate the golds. Then the mismatch won't matter." Bonnie demonstrated with a red ribbon.

"Now why didn't I think of that?" Joan slapped the counter as an *aha*. "Same reason I didn't distance myself from the gossip about my neighbor, I guess. I just didn't think. How I wish I'd spoken up the first time my friends talked about my neighbor's past. I'll bet a simple statement would have stopped the gossip. I didn't dream I'd feel so bad later. Okay, problem solver, how do I make amends to my neighbor?"

Bonnie placed a hand on Joan's arm. "Go tell her you're sorry you didn't stop the talk," she said gently. "Tell her you value her friendship. Ask her to forgive you. Then ask God to put the gossip under his blood—the blood Jesus shed on the cross hides our sin better than this strip of red will hide the mismatch of these golds."

 ## The Master Pattern

Through the blood of his Son, we are set free from our sins. God forgives our failures because of his overflowing kindness.

Ephesians 1:7

Whether our fault lies in an act we commit or in an act of omission, the blood of Jesus is available to wash it away. All we need to do is sincerely repent and ask forgiveness.

When we hurt someone else, we ask God's help to mend the relationship and humble ourselves by asking the one we injured to forgive us. Apology brings peace to our soul. The sense of being in harmony with our God is well worth the embarrassment of apologizing.

Prayer: Thank you, Jesus, for the sacrifice you made for my sins. Thank you for the blood that covers my sin and washes me clean. Help me forgive others as you forgive me. Make me quick to apologize for my failures.

Good-bye Matching

"Here are the two eggs I borrowed," Jenny said, handing the eggs to her neighbor. "Thanks so much." Before she turned to leave, a quilt top draped over the nearby sofa caught her eye. "Oh, that's a pretty quilt you're working on," she said. "What's it called?"

"Love Apple," Karen said, opening the door wider to her neighbor. "I'm giving it to my sister when she gets married." Karen motioned for Jenny to come inside and sit down.

Jenny sighed. "I wish I could make a quilt. I tried once—a Drunkard's Path pattern. I didn't enjoy it at all. I was frustrated trying to sew all those squares together and make the path pieces match properly. Most of them didn't. Then all those curved lines were hard to stitch. They curved in ways I never intended. I think in the end my Drunkard's Path was enough to drive one to drink. I gave up and I've never tried again."

Karen laughed, "You started with a difficult pattern."

"Sometimes I still dream of making a pretty quilt," Jenny admitted. "I think my daughter and the young man she's dating might get engaged, and I'd love to make a wedding quilt for them, but it would take me so long that she'd have celebrated her twenthieth anniversary by the time I finished it, not to mention my own torture in the meantime."

"Life's too short to take up a hobby you don't enjoy," Karen said. "On the other hand, I think quilting is relaxing and fulfilling." She picked up her work in progress. "I'll bet you would enjoy making an appliqué quilt. Often there isn't as much matching to do on an appliqué. The placement of the pieces doesn't have to be as exact as on pieced patterns. This Love Apple pattern would be perfect for you to try—and it's a favorite quilt for brides because of the name."

Jenny looked closer at the pattern.

"The result doesn't exactly look like an apple," Karen said, "because it's really a tomato, which was considered a love apple long ago." Karen pointed to one of the apples. "Look," she reassured Jenny, "you don't have to worry about placing the apples exactly right either. If they are a quarter inch off here or there, you won't throw off the whole piece."

"I don't know," Jenny hesitated. "I don't think I want to undertake such a big project."

"You don't have to do a whole quilt," Karen suggested. "Try doing just a wall hanging for starters. Make one big square with the center flower and four apples around it. Your daughter would think *what a nice picture* for her bedroom wall. Then, if you don't enjoy quilting, don't continue. Don't spend your time doing things you don't enjoy. There are more enjoyable things to do than we can find time for anyway."

"Does that mean I can stop cleaning the toilets?" Jenny grinned.

"Don't you wish. Sorry. The enjoy rule only applies to hobbies, or other non-necessary activities."

Jenny laughed. "Shoot, I thought you had supplied the best reason in the world to duck out of my chores."

"Too bad," Karen said. "But you know a hobby you really enjoy makes a wonderful reward to give yourself for whenever you finish your daily chores. So what do you say? Want to try quilting a wall hanging? It would be fun to work on the Love Apple together. We could pray together for our neighborhood while we stitch."

"Do you really think I could make something as pretty as your Love Apple quilt?"

"Of course," Karen said. "And if you enjoy the process, you can make a big quilt. If not, your one square will be great to hang somewhere in your daughter's house. It will convey a lot of love, because you made it with your own hands."

 ## The Master Pattern

So if you call God your Father, live your time as temporary residents on earth in fear. He is the God who judges all people by what they have done, and he doesn't play favorites.

1 Peter 1:17

We want to use wisely the time we have here on earth, following God's direction for our time. Although we desire to diligently use our time on earth in a profitable way, God knows the needs of the human body and soul for recreation and rest. He designed us so that times of refreshment would make us more productive for when we are working.

God also knows the time and practice necessary to perfect the skills he wants us to develop. When we pray about the way we use the gift of each twenty-four hours, we can enjoy the times of leisure and creativity without guilt because God uses even leisure and creativity to advance his kingdom.

Prayer: God, help me use my time according to your will. Help me find a healthy and godly balance between work and relaxation.

Stolen Kits

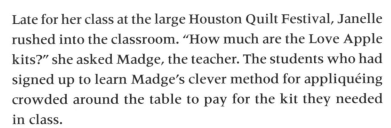

Late for her class at the large Houston Quilt Festival, Janelle rushed into the classroom. "How much are the Love Apple kits?" she asked Madge, the teacher. The students who had signed up to learn Madge's clever method for appliquéing crowded around the table to pay for the kit they needed in class.

"The Love Apple pattern is ordinarily twenty dollars," Madge said. "But today I'm offering an in-class bargain for the kit, and for every pattern you buy, I'm donating five dollars to the rebuilding fund for a church in my hometown that vandals set afire. Also I'm giving a five-dollar discount for every pattern, hoping that will enable you to buy one to increase my contribution to the church."

Madge set out a jar. "This is here if anyone can give something extra to help this burned out church. The materials for repairs are expensive."

"I read about that fire," one student said.

"What a shame," another commented.

The women chattered among themselves and stuffed money into the jar.

Janelle paid for her Love Apple quilt just as four breathless women breezed into the class and crowded up to the pattern table. Rae signed her name, paid fifteen dollars, and picked up her pattern, chatting all the while with her friends.

"Everyone take their seats," Madge tried to call the class to order. "We need to begin."

The women continued to chatter around the table, handling the samples and fabrics.

Madge tried again. "Does everyone have a kit so we can get started? We're running a little late, and I don't want you to miss any of my handy tips." She raised her voice until the women finally settled into their seats.

"See you later," one of Rae's friends waved, following another woman out the door. "We're in another class."

Madge reached for a kit to explain which pieces the students were to cut out of which colors of fabric.

"I don't understand," she said suddenly, recounting the patterns in front of her. "There are twenty people in this class and I brought twenty-six kits just in case some extra people came too. Now where did I put them?"

"Maybe some kits fell on the floor in the rush," Rae suggested.

Madge looked under the table and found one missing kit. "Now where are the other five?" she wondered aloud. Then, feeling hurried by her late start, she didn't look any further. "Take out the two curved pattern pieces for the sides of the apple," she instructed and began to show the class which pieces to cut first.

The class progressed and the women cut out their apples, stems, and leaves. Madge forgot about the missing kits and concentrated on making sure everyone learned her technique. After all, her students paid to learn appliqué, not watch her search for missing kits.

Janelle marveled at Madge's caring—how she walked around the room, helping everyone, how she was so patient to make sure each woman understood the appliquéing process. Madge knew just how to put even the most clumsy students at ease.

So when class ended, Janelle asked Madge, "May I help you clean up?"

"Thanks," Madge said. She was exhausted and relieved when the class finally ended, and she welcomed Janelle's help to pack up for home. Madge handed Janelle storage bags. "Be on the lookout for those five kits," she said. "I'm going to look over the list of who paid again. I'm positive I had twenty-six kits when I came, and I know I checked every name when each lady paid."

While Madge counted names again, Janelle shook out every bag that Madge had used to carry her supplies to the class.

Five kits still were missing.

"I hate to say it," Madge shook her head, "because quilters are such lovely, honest people, but I think someone must have taken the kits without paying."

"There was a lot of confusion with so many of us arriving late," Janelle said. "I'd like to think it was an accident, but I wonder if you are right. I was the next to last person to pay, and there were seven kits lying on the table then. When Rae paid after me, she knocked a bunch of kits on the floor. She and her friends stooped under the table, and I thought they picked them up to help. Looking back, I'm guessing her friends pocketed them."

"I never dreamed I'd need to keep a closer watch on the kits at a class like this," Madge said. "I'm so disappointed. I've never, ever been cheated at a quilt festival before." She shook her head in disbelief. "Look how generous these quilters were to contribute to the burned out church." Madge held the jar of contributions. "It hurts to think someone would steal while others were trying to help an unfortunate congregation."

"Look how generous you were to offer them the opportunity to contribute to the church and inspire them with your own example by discounting the kits," Janelle said. "It makes me mad someone would cheat you, when you are trying to help others."

"Never mind," Madge said. "I accepted this job for more reasons than to make a lot of money. I did it to increase people's enjoyment of a rewarding hobby. At the same time, I was able to help my hometown church. Even stolen kits do not take away the satisfaction of doing that. I'm going to count it a worthwhile day, and let God take care of dishonest women."

 ## The Master Pattern

Instead, store up treasures for yourselves in heaven, where moths and rust don't destroy and thieves don't break in and steal.

Matthew 6:20

When we give our hard-earned money to charitable causes, we are storing up treasure for ourselves in heaven. When we give our time and energy to help others, we are also storing up treasure. No one can steal from us what we freely give away.

Prayer: God, help me develop a generous spirit.

Copying Patterns

"I brought your mail in." Penelope examined each piece as she carried it into her neighbor's home. She held up one letter. "Why are you corresponding with Hilda? She was pie-eyed with liquor at the state fair. That reminds me. Did you read about James Joyce's scandalous book in the newspaper? He published it in France. When five hundred copies arrived here in the United States this week, the Post Office burned them. Do you know what's in that book?"

Martha ignored Penelope's prattle and question. "Thanks for bringing in the mail," she said. Penelope was the last of her neighbors to gather for an afternoon of quilting. Martha pulled a package from the mail with a smile. "Good. You can all see what I ordered from the *Sears Roebuck* catalog. This is the latest way to transfer a design to muslin for quilting. We can put it to use this afternoon."

The women gathered around as Martha opened the package. First out of the box were several patterns in stiff, thick, waxed paper with small holes punched forming various designs. She laid out two that looked like the round outline of the flowers on the Love Apple quilt top, which Martha had spread over her extended dining room table.

"Here's the new trick." Martha held up a jar and unscrewed the top to reveal a yellow paste. "The first step is to dip a cotton ball in gasoline and then rub it over this waxy paste. I'll show you how." She sent her daughter, Carrie, to the storage shed for gasoline.

Martha positioned the waxy paper with its many tiny perforated holes in between two of the appliquéd apples. She dipped the cotton ball in the gasoline, then rubbed it over the yellow substance in the jar. Next she rubbed the cotton ball over the perforated marks. Yellow dots made an outline of the design they planned to quilt on the material.

The women exclaimed approval over the system. "What a great shortcut," Carrie said.

"Using these stencils will make our design much more uniform," Martha said.

"We should have Hilda here. She could use some lessons in conforming," Penelope sniped.

The women fell silent for an awkward moment until Martha broke the silence. "Everyone, let's get this quilt marked so we can fasten it in the quilt frame and begin stitching," she said. She passed a cotton ball to each woman. For a time the women concentrated on marking their quilt.

Then conversation went from topic to topic, such as the rising popularity of the humorist Will Rogers. When someone mentioned that the House of Bishops of the Episcopal Church had eliminated the word "obey" from the marriage vows, Penelope was off on a tirade again.

"Flappers like Hilda are behind that, I'll bet!" Penelope snarked.

By the time the quilt top was marked, basted to the batting and backing layers, and then situated in the quilting frame, Martha felt frazzled trying to maintain a courteous harmony in the group. Penelope kept complaining about the Warren Harding administration. Several others kept insisting they would reserve judgment until the federal investigation into the Teapot Dome scandal was completed.

"Remember we can respectfully disagree," Martha said so often she thought she'd be saying that phrase in her sleep come night.

"I missed the last quilting bee," Penelope said. "Who did we decide was to receive this Love Apple quilt?"

Everyone looked at Martha.

"Well," Martha plucked apart a nearby cotton ball, pausing for time to think how to answer. "We decided it would be a good opportunity to show Christian love if we gave it to Hilda when she gets married next January."

"Hilda!" Penelope screeched. "Not that young whippersnapper."

"Her mother," Martha said, "is our neighbor, Penelope. We want to show Christ's love. We want to encourage Hilda to establish Christian patterns in her new home."

Martha had a headache by the time all the women left for their homes. She gathered up the perforated patterns. "This new method does make a good pattern," she told Carrie. "These marks will be easy to follow when we quilt, but setting a good pattern with our mouths for others to follow isn't as easy."

 ## The Master Pattern

Tell older women to live their lives in a way that shows they are dedicated to God. Tell them not to be gossips or addicted to alcohol, but to be examples of virtue.

Titus 2:3

Every day, our lives provide patterns of behavior that others observe. Do our patterns benefit others, if our behavior is copied, or does our behavior set a bad example? We need to exert diligence to control our tongues. Our words carry consequences. We can practice watching what we say. Wisdom will nudge us to become alert to the temptation to speak unwisely.

Prayer: God, help us to live so the patterns of our lives are worthy examples to others. Help us use our mouths wisely.

Mariner's Compass

In early American history, women's daily lives in coastal New England often centered on the work of the men at sea. The life and death of fishermen fathers, husbands, and sons hinged on the directional aid of the mariner's compass, giving this piece of equipment great importance to the watermen's women.

Magnetic compasses were first used in the late thirteenth century; quilt designs copied compass drawings that appeared on old navigation charts, especially those with a starlike figure of sixteen or thirty-two points.

Some samples of the Mariner's Compass quilts are done by patchwork piecing, but this pattern is often appliquéd. Sometimes a pattern with the arrangement of overlapping spokes emanating from a center medallion is called Rising Sun or Sunburst.

Quilts for Soldiers

"Do we have to finish this quilt today?" Betty poked her needle, threaded with white yarn, through three layers of quilt. She worked at the corner of a square of fabric from her tenth birthday dress. Even though she had outgrown the dress two years ago, she resented having to contribute it to a quilt for the Sanitary Fair.

Betty's mother, Mrs. Keene, walked down the line of chairs with girls seated around the quilting frame. "Our friends, Mary Livermore and Jan Hoge, hope you will," she said. She stopped to help one of the girls thread her needle. "They want this fair here in Chicago to be as great a success as the first one. These women know it takes a lot of money to help the soldiers."

"Why is this fair called 'Sanitary'?" Betty asked. "Is this about boiling water to sterilize stuff and washing our hands a lot?"

Her mother smiled. "Not exactly. The Sanitary Commission inspects the field medical facilities and the camp hospitals to raise the hygiene standards of our soldiers' care.

As well as assisting in the health of the sick and wounded, the organization also helps supply food. We want plenty of quilts to raise money to help the soldiers sacrificing to preserve the Union."

"I know." Betty tied her yarn into a tight knot and cut the thread short. She sighed. "But how much longer do we have to raise money for our soldiers? When the war started in 1861 all the newspapers made it sound like the war would be over in no time at all. It's 1863 and we are still making quilts for cold soldiers."

Mrs. Keene sighed. "Yes, but look how your sewing skills have improved. Next time you girls might be able to piece something more complicated like this Mariner's Compass for the soldiers." She held up the quilt she had been work-ing on for the girls to see.

"I'd like to learn how to piece the points for a Compass quilt," Judith said. "I can imagine the Compass quilt help-ing a soldier find his way home again after the war."

"That's just like you and your imagination." Betty laughed at her friend. "You need a real compass, not these scraps of fabric, to find your direction home."

"But the soldier who sleeps under your mother's Mari-ner's Compass can dream of home and pray for a safe return," Judith defended herself. "The love and prayers we stitch into our quilts can lead soldiers to think of home and pray for guidance."

Mrs. Keene patted Judith on the shoulder. "You're right. God will lead and guide us in the way that we should go."

"Besides," Judith continued to justify her fanciful thoughts, "the more lovely the quilt, the more money someone will bid on it, and the more money we'll have for the things the soldiers need."

Betty pouted nonetheless. "I still don't see why I had to cut up the prettiest dress I ever owned," she said.

"You know very well the mills are running full time and barely able to keep up supplying material for military uniforms. We can make sacrifices. We are living in our homes, instead of tents, and enjoying the heat of our fireplaces." Mrs. Keene moved closer to the warmth of the smoldering logs.

"Let's write our names on the light-colored squares," Judith said.

"May we write a letter to go with our quilt?" Betty asked.

The other girls agreed: "Good idea." "Oh, may we?"

"Maybe the soldiers will write us," Judith whispered so Mrs. Keene wouldn't hear.

"Mother, what if we write and tell President Lincoln about our Sanitary Fair? Do you think he might write us back?" Betty asked, thinking a letter from the president would make up for cutting her dress into pieces.

"Make sure we put one of our addresses on the letter to the soldier so he can find us after the war."

"Judith!" Betty tried to pretend she was shocked. "You don't want to appear forward."

"You're the one who said fabric compasses don't work like real ones," Judith said. "We'll have to give a real clue."

Mrs. Keene rolled her eyes. "You girls!"

 ## The Master Pattern

You will hear a voice behind you saying, "This is the way. Follow it, whether it turns to the right or to the left."

Isaiah 30:21

Although cloth compasses can't direct a soldier's steps, the Bible does point us to God, who desires to guide us. When life becomes difficult or even dangerous, access to God and his guidance becomes exceedingly important. If we have developed a pattern of seeking him, the Bible becomes our compass to guide our choices.

Prayer: Help me, Lord, to develop a listening ear and an understanding heart — to hear your direction for my life.

Lost and Found Squares

"Are the quilt squares I brought to the station ready for me to pick up?" Kitty asked Bernie when the man finally came on the phone. Bernie was her husband's boss at the police station.

"Quilt squares? What quilt squares?"

Kitty could hear loud voices in the background. No doubt that accounted for Bernie sounding distracted.

"You know," Kitty said. "The squares I brought for the policemen to sign in honor of Ike's retirement from the police force." Faced with silence on the other end of the phone, she began to elaborate on what she meant, a sense of panic rising in her stomach. "The ones for Ike's retirement party. I really need to finish sewing them into the quilt I'm making. I've only two weeks left until the retirement party."

She heard a sound like someone shuffling papers, a bang that could be a book falling to the ground, followed by a whisper she couldn't decipher.

"I can't seem to find them. What did they look like?"

Kitty always did think Bernie's voice sounded like the scratch of lemon on a kitchen grater. "Just plain muslin squares with a note and a fabric pen for signing them."

"Nope, not on my desk."

Kitty's nerves felt grated at the gravely pitch of Bernie's tone.

"They shouldn't be on your desk." Kitty worked to bring the pitch of her voice down to a controlled level. "You've had them for several months. They should have been distributed to the policemen who work with my husband for their signatures."

"Here, I'll connect you with my secretary. She should know more."

Kitty heard the click that signaled Bernie had transferred her call. Waiting for the connection, she poured out her frustration to another librarian on her staff: "I've sent and received autographed squares all over the world; even students from Denmark and Australia, who stayed in our home as foreign exchange students, have signed and returned them. Yet I can't get a few squares back from the police precinct less than one mile from my home!"

"I'm sorry, Mrs. Orland." Brenda, Bernie's secretary, came on the line before Kitty had finished her tirade. "What's the problem?"

"Oh, dear, I shouldn't be spouting off. It's not your fault, Brenda, but I need the quilt squares I brought to the precinct for personal signatures. It's going to take lots of time to sew those squares into the Mariner's Compass quilt I'm making Ike. The squares are signed, aren't they?" Kitty heard shrill panic in her voice.

"Tell you what," Brenda said. "I'll look around and see what I can find and call you back. Okay, Mrs. Orland?"

After Brenda hung up, Kitty spread out the partially completed quilt. The top squares needed to be balanced on the bottom by the ones from the precinct. As she admired the blue and yellow sashing between the squares, and how it carried the colors of the central Mariner's Compass throughout the quilt, she fretted. "I should have called and reminded the station more often," she scolded herself.

Before she had time to cut out more sashing strips, Brenda called back. "I found your squares and the men have signed them," she announced.

"Oh, good." Kitty let out a sigh of relief. "Where were they hiding?"

"Well, they weren't exactly hiding. They were in the duty room in a box with a sign attached that said, 'The sergeant's wife is making Ike a quilt. Please sign a fabric square and return to the box.'"

"Isn't the duty room open to everyone?" Kitty asked in dismay. "This quilt is supposed to be a surprise."

"Oh, dear," Brenda sympathized. "Everybody goes to the duty room over and over throughout the day. I'll put the box in my car now and hope Ike hasn't seen it yet. You know some men aren't very observant about something that doesn't directly affect them." Brenda hoped Ike was one of those unobservant-in-the-office types.

To Kitty's delight, weeks later, Ike's mouth dropped open in genuine surprise when she presented the quilt at his retirement party. "A Mariner's Compass pattern, you say?" he said. "Perfect. My dream for retirement is to do lots of sailing."

"You didn't suspect something from the sign requesting autographs in the duty room?"

"I never saw a sign asking for autographs," Ike said. "Where was it?"

 ## The Master Pattern

> I have made an agreement with my eyes.
>
> Job 31:1

> Then let God weigh me on honest scales, and he will know I have integrity.
>
> Job 31:6

If Ike had seen the sign announcing what his wife was making for him, it would have spoiled the delightful element of surprise, but the sight would not have caused him any harm.

However, the world offers tempting sights for our eyes which can lead us into harm. Our eyes open the gates to many temptations: coveting, gluttony, and sexual sin. We can protect ourselves by making a pact to not allow our eyes to linger on the sights that tempt us. We gain integrity and avoid trouble by the small, daily choices we make.

Prayer: Help me guard my soul by using discipline about what I allow my eyes to gaze upon.

The Last Stitch

The afternoon was drawing to a close, and the women were getting hot as the sun poured into Thelma Brown's parlor and onto the quilting frame upon which the church ladies leaned. Tempers also warmed up between the ladies.

"I hear Jeff's courting my niece, Lily," Mrs. Ramon said, quilting around the Mariner's Compass closest to her.

"I doubt that," Sadie replied. "He bought *my* lunch at the church social." Sadie put down her needle to challenge Mrs. Ramon's statement.

Mrs. Ramon stopped sewing also. "Lily won first prize with her pickles at the fair," she said, trying to change the subject.

"So my pickles turned out soggy. What's that to do with courting?"

"You make the flakiest pie crust, Sadie." Thelma tried to turn the conversation. "Speaking of pies, are the apples on your farm ready for picking, Leah?" Thelma thumped the star pattern next to Mrs. Ramon, trying in vain to catch her eye.

"Nearly ready," Leah said. "Do you want some for pies?" Leah quilted around one point.

"Who bought your lunch at the church social, Leah?" Sadie asked.

Leah lowered her head and didn't answer.

"Did any young man buy your lunch?" Mrs. Ramon pursued Sadie's lead.

"My, look how the sun is lowering." Thelma tried again to rescue the atmosphere of the quilting bee. "It's time for us older women to take a recess. Here, let me help you up." She took Mrs. Ramon's arm, tugged her to her feet, and guided her to the kitchen so fast that Mrs. Ramon nearly stumbled. "Remember our usual custom," Thelma said, winking. "As we older women rest and make a fresh pot of coffee, the younger single ladies will finish the quilt. The border is all that's left. The girl who puts in the last stitch will be the first one to marry."

The single girls repositioned themselves around the quilt so each had an equal amount of the border to quilt, then sat down again. They began to stitch, but slowly, trying to look industrious in spite of their deliberate, pokey sewing.

"I don't know about the wisdom of our custom today," Mrs. Ramon said as she measured coffee into the pot.

Thelma put out fresh cups. "You're right. Those girls are such rivals that each one of them may quilt at a snail's pace so as to get in the last stitch."

"But we need to get the Mariner's Compass quilt done by the time the circuit-riding pastor arrives," Mrs. Ramon said.

"That's just next week." Thelma shook her head. " Look at those girls. Eight-year-olds could quilt faster." She stopped at the sound of a buggy outside.

Lily tied her horse to a post and hurried into the house. "Sorry, I missed most of this quilting bee," she gushed. "I was helping Mrs. Marshall with sick twins." She took off her bonnet. "Thought I'd help, even if late, to make sure we get the quilt done on time. It makes a good 'thank you' for the circuit rider."

"That's right," Sadie said. But she thought, *Isn't it just like you to come too late to do much of anything except make the last stitch.*

Leah moved over to make room for Lily. Sadie caught sight of a small tear in the corner of Leah's eye.

Sadie's sympathies stirred. "We all like Pastor Ryner and want to finish his quilt," Sadie said. "We'd better get moving. Pastor is always telling us about first John, chapter four, where the Bible says, 'Beloved, if God so loved us, we ought also to love one another.'" She nodded her head toward Leah, whose eyes concentrated on her stitching. Every line of Leah's posture demonstrated her dejected attitude.

Lily picked up Sadie's intention. "Come on, girls, let's get this done." Lily began to sew for all she was worth.

"Yes, let's." Sadie set up a fast tempo of rocking her needle through the layers. The other girls picked up their speed also.

"Beloved, let us love one another." Sadie began to sing the familiar Bible chorus and the other girls all joined in: "For love is of God; and every one that loveth is born of God, and knoweth God."

One girl after another finished the section in front of her, knotted her thread, and cut it off.

All the girls grinned as Leah continued sewing, singing along with them, unaware she was the last one still quilting. Leah reached the end of her row and looked up.

"You made the last stitch," one of the girls told Leah. "You'll be the next one of us to marry."

A smile hesitated at the corner of Leah's mouth. "But no one even tried to buy my box lunch." Her voice quavered.

"The fellows haven't caught on to what a treasure you are," Sadie said. "Look at what an industrious wife you'll make."

Leah's face brightened.

"Tell you what," Lily offered, "I'll put some of my pickles in your lunch the next box social we have."

"I'll help you fix some curls around your face," Sadie said, pulling a wisp of Leah's hair from behind one ear and curling it around her little finger. "See how pretty Leah is."

Leah's smile grew wider.

"Well, I'll be." Mrs. Ramon put her coffee cup down. "Who would have dreamed how proud we can be of those young 'uns."

 ## The Master Pattern

Love each other as I have loved you. This is what I'm commanding you to do.

John 15:12

To love the same way God loves us requires putting others' interests ahead of our own. Even a glimpse of God's amazing love for us is enough to revolutionize how we treat others and how we feel about ourselves. God's love transforms us.

Prayer: God, deepen our comprehension of your great, all-encompassing love for us. Give each one of us such a grasp of your love that it changes every fiber of our being.

Rescued Quilt

"According to the news reports, our neighborhood was hit hard by the hurricane." Clyde Johnson glanced at Sophia as they drove toward the home they had evacuated when the Category Four hurricane advanced upon their community.

"I know." Sophia twisted her sweater.

"Steel yourself, honey. It may not be a pretty sight."

"Devastating" was Sophia's word when they turned the corner. The Johnsons' home looked like a Lego building that children had thrown across the room. Clyde pulled to a stop in front of a fallen tree across the driveway.

Sophia buried her head in his shoulder. For long minutes they clung to one another in front of the destruction. "I can't believe this," Sophia finally spoke between sobs. "Everything is torn up." She waved at the mess. "This looks like a giant had a temper tantrum."

"A giant storm for sure." Clyde climbed out of the car and slammed his fist against the hood. "What a mess!" He kicked a garbage can out of the way and walked around to open the door on Sophia's side.

"What will we do?" Sophia reached for a tissue.

"We might as well look around for what we can salvage. If we find small things we can put them in the car." Clyde took Sophia's hand and led her carefully around the tree debris to the house.

He stopped just outside the dangling front door. "Look, here's the end table your father made us. It's in fine condition." Clyde set it upright on the sidewalk.

Sophia walked inside and poked her finger into a cushion sodden with rain. "The sofa and upholstered chairs are ruined." Her dreams lay in ruins around her too.

"Let's focus on what we can salvage," Clyde soothed. "Our insurance will help us replace things."

"Not the irreplaceable, sentimental losses."

Clyde swallowed hard. "At least we loaded our picture albums into the car when we evacuated. We have those."

Clyde and Sophia made their way into what had been the kitchen. The cabinets were torn from the wall and rested across the room.

"Look here." Clyde stood in front of the sink. "The counters are every which way, yet the dishes in the sink aren't even broken."

Sophia clutched a plate to her chest. "I can't believe it. We have two complete place settings in the sink, completely unharmed."

"Be careful where you step," Clyde cautioned. "A whole section of the kitchen floor is torn loose and turned on its side."

"But look what's underneath it," Sophia perked up. "Our crystal."

"And it's not broken." Clyde picked up a piece, "How on earth did the crystal remain undamaged, yet the floor get all torn up?"

"I can hardly believe it," Sophia said, smiling. "Thank you, Jesus."

Together, Sophia and Clyde retrieved some dish towels from a drawer and began to carefully wrap the fragile crystal goblets and pile them in the sink with the unbroken dishes. So much crystal was in good condition, they soon filled the double sinks to the top. With lighter hearts, they continued their search for what they could retrieve.

"Would you look!" Clyde tossed aside some uprooted flooring. "Here's something you'll be glad to see." He held up a quilt top.

"Oh," Sophia said, truly moved. "That's the Mariner's Compass quilt top Grandma Poyner made, but never quilted." Sophia unfolded the quilt. "The fabric looks a little discolored in some places, but I don't care. I'm so happy to have something she made." Sophia hugged the damp quilt to her. "What a special reminder of my wonderful grandma." Sophia handed one end of the quilt top to Clyde. "Help me fold it," she said. "As soon as we get this mess cleaned up, I'm going to quilt this. Finishing Grandma's quilt will help me remember to be thankful for the treasures that were spared, instead of groaning about the losses. Every time I want to grieve over our loss, I'll stitch a bit."

 ## The Master Pattern

He is not afraid of bad news.
　　His heart remains secure, full of confidence in the LORD.

Psalm 112:7

Over and over, throughout history, people have faced devastating property loss because of fire, storm, war, or evil people. In every instance that we face tragedy in any form, we face a decision: How will we respond?

Shock, despair, discouragement, and anger are natural responses.

Every person must work his or her way through the bombardment of emotions that accompanies loss; in the end, being confident in the Lord, as Psalm 112 exhorts, brings wholeness to our souls. Confidence in the Lord is worth the battle.

Pray for God to fill us with confidence in him to see us through disasters, into better days. The ultimate truth is that without God, nothing else matters. With God, all kinds of redemption and restoration are possible. He knows our dreams for our lives.

Prayer: God, give us strong confidence in you. Assure us that you can take anything that happens to us and bring good from it. Become our security above every natural security.

Rose of Sharon

This pattern is based on Song of Songs 2:1, which refers to Jesus, saying, "I am the rose of Sharon, a lily, growing, in the valleys." Sharon is the name of a valley in Palestine, referenced in the Old Testament, and the rose refers to a wild tulip that still grows there on the plains.

Since the eighteenth century this lovely pattern has enjoyed growing popularity. The arrangement of the flowers, buds, and leaves varies in design, but the colors are often rose, green, and gold. The Rose of Sharon pattern—also called Whig Rose for the Whig political party in the 1828 election—was especially popular in the mid-nineteenth century. Since the rose symbolizes love and marriage, this quilt pattern is frequently made for newlyweds.

Protected Stitches

"No, no!" Diane waved a newspaper at Gigi, the cocker spaniel who was rubbing her back on a quilt Diane proudly hung in her front hall. "Grandma made that quilt. Don't you dare get it dirty or rub grass off on it."

Gigi tucked her tail between her legs and ran into the kitchen.

"Oh dear! Carl, come look at this." Diane knelt to inspect the bottom border of the Rose of Sharon quilt. "One of the grandchildren has written 'Jesus' with a Magic Marker on Grandma's quilt."

Her husband, Carl, rounded the corner. "I wondered where the front section was." He retrieved his newspaper from his wife and squatted to look at the quilt.

"Well, a lot worse words could have been written there." The corner of Carl's mouth quirked with the hint of a smile. "At least one of our grandchildren connects this pattern to Jesus."

"I'll bet it was Josh," Diane said. "I told him about some of the names of Jesus last weekend and showed him this quilt when he asked what was a Rose of Sharon anyway. The little rascal!"

Diane and Carl both smiled, remembering the lively antics of Josh, who kept their home in a swirl of activity whenever they took care of him.

"He's so happy with school this year that he does seem to write on anything handy," Carl said, chuckling. "A lot of my tools carry his autograph."

"So do all the magazines on the end table. Oh well, better the magazines than the wood of the table."

"Does Magic Marker come off?" Carl rubbed the intruding marks with his finger.

"Well, there are washable markers," Diane said, already heading to the kitchen for cleaning supplies. "Maybe I can just spot it with something to make it less noticeable. I don't want to wash the whole quilt. It's old and fragile and valuable, at least to me. Think of all the hours Grandma spent making these roses and vines for my parents' wedding present. This quilt is irreplaceable, really; it represents the hopes and dreams Grandma had for my parents' marriage."

Diane used a soft-bristled brush to remove Gigi's hair from the green leaf sections on the quilt. "I'll look up the best way to wash marker from an old quilt." She retrieved her quilt care book from the bookcase.

Carl looked over her shoulder. "I suppose we're fortunate that Gigi only rubbed instead of chewed."

"Good point. I guess we should take it down now that we have a puppy and the grandchildren have moved close enough for us to babysit. I'll miss its cheerful presence in our hall."

"Maybe you won't have to take it down." Carl put the edge of his hand against the wall at the side of the quilt. "A Plexiglas protector over the bottom foot or so would do the trick. I'll use spacers and washers to hold the Plexiglas out from the wall. That way the protective shield won't rest against the quilt, but will still prevent danger from Gigi or kids who act as rambunctious as pups."

 ## The Master Pattern

But you, O Lord, are a shield that surrounds me.
You are my glory.
You hold my head high.

Psalm 3:3

He will cover you with his feathers,
and under his wings you will find refuge.
His truth is your shield and armor.

Psalm 91:4

What a comfort to know God is our shield. Whether we're dealing with a matter that's small, such as a quilt, or as great as physical danger, God surrounds us with his protection. We can rest in the truth that his security offers greater defense than anything the world offers.

In the midst of protecting us from whatever threatens us, he will help us hold up our heads high too. We need not bow with shame or discouragement before the threats of the enemy, whether they take the form of physical or emotional threats. Instead, we bow before God and listen to his wisdom for counsel to avoid unnecessary dangers, and we submit to his truths as our final authority. He will guide us.

Prayer: Lord, surround me with your shield of protection over my mind, my thinking, and my body.

Winning Stitches

"She isn't good enough for our family, Benny." Dora didn't try to lower her voice.

"Shh, mom. Ellie will hear you." Ben put a restraining hand on his mother's shoulder.

"I don't care if she does." Dora walked away from him. "What were you thinking marrying a common girl like Ellie? She's beneath us."

Stunned, Ellie stood still outside the door to the kitchen.

Dora continued her rant. "Her family doesn't have a profession."

Ben tried to defend Ellie. "Give her a chance, Mother," he said. "You'll love her, if you take the time to get to know her. Please don't upset her by calling her names and putting down her family—they are honorable people."

Ellie's scowl at Dora's words relaxed. *My parents are hard-working. What a mean, spiteful woman,* Ellie thought. For her husband's sake, she smiled before entering the kitchen for breakfast, pretending she hadn't heard a thing.

Ben looked at her frozen smile and knew differently. He reached out and hugged Ellie. "Keep the peace, my darling, for

189

my sake," he whispered in her ear, then pulled back to look at her face, before pulling out a chair for her. "I love you," he said out loud as much for his mother's benefit as his wife's.

Ellie poured milk on her oatmeal, wondering if it would curdle when it landed in her stomach, which was roiling with resentment. Her thoughts seethed as she forced down some cereal and listened to Dora's conversation.

"My best friend, Lanie, bought a diamond brooch to wear on her gown for the abolitionist ball next month. Lanie told me her daughter will be escorted to the ball by the son of our New Hampshire governor, so she might buy a smaller diamond brooch for her daughter's gown."

"I thought the idea of the ball was to raise money for the abolitionist cause, not to spend money on fancy baubles," Ben said.

Dora ignored his remark and rambled on, "When I last called on Lanie, she showed me two appliquéd quilts. You can tell Lanie is a lady of leisure and wealth to own two such quilts. They are beautiful and the needlework is exquisite. Imagine having time enough for such intricate work! What a skill."

Ellie nearly sputtered her coffee. She restrained herself from retorting that she could appliqué quilt tops with the best of folks. Her next thought made her stiffen her back: *Appliqué my snobbish mother-in-law a quilt? Not on your life.* But by the time breakfast was over, Ellie had a design in mind and even planned the colors she wanted to use to blend with her mother-in-law's bedroom.

When Ellie asked for money to buy muslin, she announced, "I'm going to make your mother a Rose of Sharon quilt."

Ben raised his eyebrows in disbelief.

"The muslin is all I'll need to buy. I'll cut up my old yellow gown for the roses and use the good sections of an old green tablecloth for the leaves and stems."

"You'll go to all that trouble and take all that time after what Mother said at breakfast?" Ben gathered his wife in his arms.

Ellie snuggled close. "Well, she admires appliqué and thinks owning an appliqué quilt would give her status. If she thinks appliqué will improve what people think of her, I can give her what she wants, for all it's worth."

Ellie set about making the quilt and with every stitch, she prayed for Dora. Hours of prayer, as Ellie plied her needle around roses, stems, and leaves, softened her toward Ben's mother. By the time she fastened the pattern to the muslin with tiny stitches, tiny seeds of love took root in Ellie's attitude.

When Ellie presented the finished quilt to her mother-in-law, Dora stood stock still. Ellie watched an array of emotions sweep across her mother-in-law's face. At first Ellie saw the customary disdain blended with resentment. Then she watched as a look of disbelief slowly turned to a smile on Dora's lips and began to spread to her eyes.

To the amazement of both of them, Dora slowly reached out her arms to Ellie in a hug, her smile as warm as the quilt she crushed between them.

 ## The Master Pattern

But I tell you this: Love your enemies, and pray for those who persecute you. In this way you

show that you are children of your Father in
heaven.

Matthew 5:44–45

Ellie began her Rose of Sharon quilt because of her love
for her husband. In the process of giving and praying, she
ended with an attitude change as well as earning appreciation from her mother-in-law.

Spending time in prayer helps how we respond to nega-
tive people. Sometimes we gain insights into what makes a
person hostile or difficult. While we may not cause people
around us to change their ingrained patterns, our way of
life can soften a person if we plant acceptance and love,
two necessities that every person craves.

*Prayer: Lord, please help me to love people with your love
even when they are unlovable. Help me demonstrate love
and acceptance to those whose lives have left them lacking
in those needs.*

Honoring Stitches

Dana checked her reflection in the mirror outside the hotel ballroom. She turned sideways to check her profile, sucking in her stomach. "Do you think this dress makes me look fat?" she asked her husband.

"No." Alan suppressed a sigh. "Same answer as when you tried it on in the store. Same answer as when you tried it one more time before packing it in the suitcase." He put his arm around her waist. "Hmm, still look great to me. Are you sure it wouldn't be more fun to go back up to our hotel room instead of to your high school reunion?" He breathed heavily into her ear.

Dana gave him a playful smack. "My high school girlfriends were all a bunch of skinny minnies ten years ago. I know I've gained weight, but I don't want to look fat."

Alan took her hand. "You've gained three babies and a few well-earned pounds. While you are stewing by this mirror, I've watched a good number of 'mature' figures enter the ballroom. You look beautiful. Come on, Dreamboat, let's go wow the gang."

"Wow" was the first word Dana said, entering the ballroom. A gorgeous quilt hung in a prominent place by the door.

"Three dollars for a raffle ticket and a chance to win this quilt," a woman called.

Dana cried in delight as she recognized the woman as Kathy, her study partner through four years of high school math.

"You look wonderful," Kathy reached for a hug before explaining the raffle. "The money for the quilt is going to the Heart Association for research in honor of Sharon Delmar."

"I read about Sharon's death in the newsletter," Dana said. "I never suspected she had heart trouble. She and I had the best times together, running out our hearts on the basketball court." Dana stopped at the implication of her words. "Do you think her heart wasn't all right back when we were on the team?"

"No one suspected trouble until after college," Kathy said. "Deb, Alice, and I decided to make a quilt to honor her memory. We hope the donations will make a dent in understanding heart disease."

"It's beautiful," Dana said, filling out a raffle form. She read the top of the form. " 'Pattern called Rose of Sharon.' What a perfect pattern for Sharon. The rose was her favorite flower." Dana looked at the bright yellow flowers appliquéd on a lovely rose-colored background.

"I wish she were here and we could trade memories." Dana felt a pang of loss.

"Sit at my table." Kathy pointed to one nearby. "We'll trade war stories about memorizing theorems and formulas in the girl's bathroom and rehearsing them together until the very last minute before our tests."

Dana finished filling out the form, and Alan opened his wallet to pull out some bills and tuck them into the raffle jar. He reached for his wife's hand and led her to the table Kathy indicated.

Dana was delighted later that evening when she learned that she won the quilt. She went forward to collect her prize as her classmates called, "Speech, speech."

"Every time I look at this quilt, I'll always remember dribbling down the basketball court with Sharon," she told the group. "I'll think of the good times I had sharing dreams of the future with Kathy, Deb, and Alice. I want to thank them for their thoughtfulness to take the time to make such a fitting memorial to Sharon. We are a fortunate class, with many wonderful memories. I don't know if I realized the importance of relationships when I was in school; but now, especially when we think of Sharon, we will always remember her kindness and interest in us. I think we all want to be remembered for our love and caring too. I love you guys."

Dana's classmates applauded while she walked back to her seat, and Dana didn't think even once to suck in her stomach.

 ## The Master Pattern

Teach us to number each of our days so that we may grow in wisdom.

Psalm 90:12

The days of our lives brim over with the trivia of living. Wisdom reminds us that love is the most important treasure we collect on this earth. When someone's death jolts the rhythm of our days, we are reminded that no one has a guarantee or any idea of how long we will live.

Wisdom dismisses the unimportant and packs each day with love. We have a choice. We can choose to dwell on the trivial or we can choose to contribute love to the lives of those we encounter.

Prayer: Prevent me from majoring in the trivia of life and help me focus on loving others.

Trading Hoes for Spindles

Louise threaded the broken rope of combed fiber under the machine's feeder. She knew the mechanism would mend the break before the fiber wound onto the spindle. Then the closing bell rang at the Lowell mill, breaking her concentration.

Louise leaned against the spindle table. "My legs feel like rubber," she told Ira, the mill girl who worked closest to her. "I wonder how many miles I've walked checking all these spindles." She gestured toward the one hundred or more spindles wound with fiber in readiness for the next step of making raw cotton into fabric.

"I don't think I've ever had so many breaks in the ropes as I did today." Ira exercised her fingers, opening and closing her fists. "The girls on the combing machines must not be monitoring the fiber properly before it reaches us. I never saw so many weak places."

Louise took off her apron and hung it on a hook. "Staying at high alert has worn me out," she said. "Seems like all I did was fix breaks. Actually, I'd rather tire out watching

197

for breaks and weak spots than lean over tomato plants in the hot sun back home on the farm, watching for big, fat tomato bugs. I hated plucking off those nasty bugs."

"I guess I'd choose weak threads over tomato bugs too," Ira agreed. "Maybe I'll skip class tonight." She replaced one last spindle and turned toward the door. "Are you going to class?"

"Sure. I'm not any more tired than when I hoed a field of corn on Daddy's farm, and I didn't get paid for my work there." Louise untied the scarf tied around her head and shook free her blonde curls. "I'm glad for the classes. I've learned a lot about proper English and writing business letters. I don't plan to run around checking fiber spindles all my life in this textile mill." The sparkle of dreams shone in Louise's eyes.

"Me neither," Ira said, skipping a step to match Louise's gait. "Every week, I choose a book from all those volumes in the library. I never saw so many books in one place before. Widow Johnson says books open doors to the future."

"Mr. Lowell did a good thing starting his Lowell System for this mill, so that we could come here and work with supervised care while earning money. I'm saving money just like our house mother requires, and I still have some money left to send home to my little sister, Anne. She wrote to me that she's saving for a piano."

Mrs. Johnson, the boarding house chaperone, practically fluttered as she greeted the girls returning from work. "Girls." She used her most commanding voice. "Supper will be quick tonight, and classes are suspended. Tomorrow, President Andrew Jackson is coming to visit our Waltham Mill as part of the Lowell Mill System."

Mrs. Johnson smiled at the collective gasps from the mill girls. "Give your rooms a thorough cleaning and make sure you press your clothes for tomorrow. We want the president to see how lovely our place is and what good work you girls do. Remember, curfew is 10:00 p.m. as always."

"Tell the carding machine girls to do good work so we don't have a series of fiber breaks to show the president." Ira spoke so only Louise could hear.

The frequent breaks in the fiber that day became the major topic of dinner conversation. No one wanted President Andrew Jackson to have an unfavorable impression of their mill.

"Don't point blame at others," Mrs. Johnson said. "Think instead of the weaknesses in your own life that make you break under pressure."

"Maybe someone should start a Lowell magazine with articles that tell about the life principles we learn here at the mill," one of the girls responded to Mrs. Johnson's mini-sermon.

"I'll write an article about 1 Thessalonians 5:14," Ira volunteered. "That Bible verse says something about encouraging people who are idle or timid, helping weak people, and being patient with everyone."

Someone could write an article each quarter about ways to use the fabric we make here at Lowell, Louise thought. Then her idea bloomed. "I'll write an article about the Rose of Sharon quilt I'm working on," she announced. "I started it at home, but now girls in other departments have given me lots of pretty scraps from the mill. I can tell how they helped me finish it faster!"

The Master Pattern

And he said unto me, My grace is sufficient for thee: for my strength is made perfect in weakness. Most gladly therefore will I rather glory in my infirmities, that the power of Christ may rest upon me.

2 Corinthians 12:9 KJV

God knows how to take the breaks in our life and mend them so our weaknesses become a way for others to see the power of God working through us. When we see God using what we know used to be our weakness, it is easier to bear with the failings of others.

Those of us who have strong faith must be patient with the weaknesses of others whose faith is not so strong, according to Romans 15:1. We must not think only of ourselves.

Prayer: God, help me be patient with the weaknesses of others. Instead of criticizing them, help me turn to you. Turn my weaknesses into your strength.

Wandering Foot

In early America, the Wandering Foot quilt pattern carried the superstition that a child who slept under it would leave home too soon and become a wanderer. No parent wanted this.

To sidestep the superstition, some quilters simply changed the pattern's name to Turkey Tracks, since wild turkeys roaming the forests were a common sight in colonial America. The new name made the pattern acceptable.

Another name attached to the pattern was Iris Leaf, when appliquéd with green fabrics; the first pattern of this design was called Tents of Kedar for nomadic tribes from Bible days.

Sacrificed Stitches

"Everyone, quick. Grab old quilts and sheets and run to the garden." Mother rushed into the log cabin from out back.

"What is it?" Hetty looked up from stitching her first alphabet sampler.

"Grasshoppers are coming. Hurry, I see a big cloud of hoppers on the horizon."

Tommy, the oldest, understood his mother's urgency. He ran to strip his bed and dashed into the garden.

"Hetty, you can finish sewing later. Quick, take this quilt and throw it over the rows of peas." Mother pulled a quilt from a chest and thrust it into Hetty's arms. "Go on."

Hetty was shocked. "This isn't old. It's the Wandering Foot quilt Aunt Ethel gave Sammy when he was born."

"Quick." Mother was frantic, giving Hetty a shove toward the door. "Throw it over the rows of peas. It's wide enough to cover a lot."

Hetty still hesitated. "Won't the grasshoppers eat our quilts? This one is new."

"Good riddance, if they do. Now go." Mother ran along-side her daughter with several quilts in her arms. "I will never allow Sammy to sleep under it, anyway."

In a short time the whole family—Mother, Hetty, sister Matilda, and the boys—were outside stretching sheets and quilts over the vegetable garden.

Father galloped out of the nearest field on the back of Chestnut, the bay; at the cabin, he swung off before the horse slid to a complete stop.

"Grasshoppers," he yelled, "Swarms and swarms of them." He saw the quilts and nodded toward them. "Good thinking. At least we can save the vegetables, but I don't see any hope for the cornfields."

"Isn't there anything we can do for the corn?" Mother looked toward the fast-approaching cloud of insects.

"The boys and I can run up and down the rows waving hats and dish towels to knock off the hoppers. Probably futile, but let's try, boys."

Tommy scooped up dish towels. Ralph swung George and Billy onto Chestnut and smacked his rump. Tommy and Ralph ran after them into the field.

"Won't the hoppers get under our quilts and sheets?" Hetty asked.

"They're well overlapped," Mother said, looking around. "But, quick, gather stones, and we'll hold the outside edges to the ground with rocks. Some hoppers will get under but we probably can save most of the vegetables."

Across the field, the girls saw the great cloud of grasshoppers drop into the cornfield. The boys ran up and down flapping their hats and towels.

The girls and Mother ran into the house, slamming the door against the invasion of chomping insects.

"Why won't you let Sammy sleep under the Wandering Foot quilt?" Hetty asked over the buzz of the grasshoppers.

"I didn't want to hurt Aunt Ethel's feelings when she made a Wandering Foot quilt for Sammy, but I don't want him sleeping under it and wandering from home at a young age." Mother shook her head. "No. Better to use Auntie's gift to save our peas and beans from the grasshoppers. That way her gift puts food in Sammy's belly. Don't guess she knew it was a Wandering Foot pattern when she made it." Mother dropped to her knees and prayed until the destroying swarm suddenly lifted and changed direction as quickly as it had arrived.

As the cloud passed over the horizon, she and the girls then peeled away the quilts and sheets from their garden. Only a few grasshoppers were munching on the plants, but the girls swatted until the last one was dead or flew away, leaving the rows of lush green leaves mostly undisturbed. Dad and the boys came in, dragging their dishtowels on the ground.

"The grasshoppers ate all the tender leaves," Dad said. "The corn crop is gone. We'll cut the field and make a haystack from what's left. When the stalks dry, at least they will make fodder for the animals to eat."

"But what will we eat?" Hetty asked.

"God will supply." Dad's strong voice belied his drooping shoulders.

"We'll eat from our vegetable garden," Mother said, putting an arm around each of her girls. "Your quick work saved it."

 ## The Master Pattern

Then I will repay you for the years that the mature locusts, the adult locusts, the grasshoppers, and the young locusts ate your crops.

Joel 2:25

I have been young, and now I am old, but I have never seen a righteous person abandoned or his descendants begging for food.

Psalm 37:25

We can trust God to supply our needs. We may need to redefine what we need and distinguish needs from wants, but even in lean times, God cares for us.

Prayer: God, we thank you for your promise to provide for us. We ask you to restore whatever the locusts have devoured in our lives. In addition to the material things we need, we ask you to restore relationships, hopes, and dreams as well.

Restore

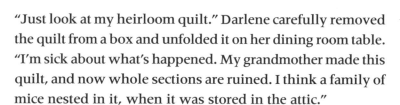

"Just look at my heirloom quilt." Darlene carefully removed the quilt from a box and unfolded it on her dining room table. "I'm sick about what's happened. My grandmother made this quilt, and now whole sections are ruined. I think a family of mice nested in it, when it was stored in the attic."

"The colors are beautiful." Carol ran a finger over a deep green curve ending with three-pronged, yellow leaves at each corner of the square. "What's this pattern called?"

"Grandmother called it Wandering Foot. She made it for her firstborn son, Frank. The day after he graduated from high school, without consulting his parents, Frank took a job with the railroad. Mother said she had never seen Grandma so agitated as when Frank told about his new job. Right then, Grandma boxed up the quilt and put it in the attic, and within the week, Uncle Frank was rattling down the tracks to tote luggage in and out of baggage cars wherever the train stopped. Poor Grandma never did adjust to the fact his work took him all over the United States. She mourned whenever he missed important events and

holidays. Never mind that Uncle Frank said he was fulfilling a dream."

"What did that have to do with the quilt?" Carol said.
"Wait," she answered herself. "I'll bet your grandmother
thought he had a wanderlust to travel and see the country
because of this quilt."

"You got it," Darlene said. "Lots of people held the superstition that to sleep under a Wandering Foot quilt pattern
made a person want to wander away from home. In fact,
women often called the pattern Turkey Tracks, hoping to
prevent a child from leaving the area."

Carol laughed, "I'd put a Turkey Track quilt on Sam's bed
if I thought it would make him stay in Tennessee."

"I'd sleep under this quilt, holes and all, if I thought I
could see some of the wonderful sights Uncle Frank de-
scribed when he came home for visits," Darlene said. "But
seriously, it is about the only memento I have of my grandmother. Do you have any ideas for how I could make it into
something useful?"

With caution, Carol pulled back another fold of the
quilt."There are plenty of good sections left. Maybe you
could make a vest out of the good parts."

"Maybe. But I'd feel mighty nervous cutting into Grandma's handiwork."

"The mice didn't suffer from such scruples." Carol shook
her head at the quilt's condition. "But there are good
places. Look, this section is big enough for the back of
a vest."

Darlene nodded. "It's ruined for use as a quilt. I was
only joking about sleeping under a mouse-eaten quilt so
I could travel the United States. I wouldn't really put this

chomped-up quilt on my bed." She nodded at Carol. "Let's do it. You'll help me, won't you?"

Several times, Carol rescued the project. Darlene was ready to quit when she cut one of the front pieces much shorter and narrower than the other.

"Never mind," Carol reassured. "There are no mistakes when you're making something—only opportunity for creative expression you didn't know you had." She tipped her head to survey the two uneven pieces. "Let's cut a very wide strip and sew it to the small side of the vest to make it the same size as the other." Carol held up a piece to show the effect.

"What about the other side? Won't that look funny and unbalanced?"

"Not at all. If you embroider around the leaves on the other edge, it will look as if you planned it to appear asymmetrical."

"I guess if the final appearance is pretty, no one will ever know I made a mistake." Darlene began to cut the wide strip.

"You know, working with the railroad was not a mistake for Uncle Frank. He noticed that train stations weren't always in the best sections of town, because rich people didn't want the noise and dirt of the coal-burning engines near their fancy homes. When Uncle Frank noticed that hungry children were at every train station, he began carrying boxes of canned goods and bags of flour and sugar. He gave them to the kids attracted by the noisy whistle of the train stopping for a few minutes in their towns. He organized food programs where the trains made lengthy stops. Although Grandma missed him terribly, his work gave him a sense of accomplishment, like fulfilling a dream he didn't even know he had." Darlene pinned a strip of the quilt cloth onto the smaller vest piece.

Carol was right. The light green embroidery around and over the yellow leaves looked beautiful. Working a blanket stitch with the same color embroidery thread down the edge of the wide strip balanced the visual effect.

Darlene finished the vest and wore it with joy. She loved remembering how her grandmother handled the pretty material and carefully stitched the beautiful pattern. Most of all she loved the quilted vest's warmth around her body—it reminded her that God's love could take the dreams life had chewed to pieces and create something of beauty and purpose.

 ## The Master Pattern

> We know that all things work together for the good of those who love God—those whom he has called according to his plan.
>
> Romans 8:28

God didn't make a mistake when he created us. We are each a creative masterpiece from the hand of the ultimate creator. When we make mistakes as we live our lives, we can go to God and ask him to bring something good from our blunders. He is the master of repair. He can take our ruined cloth, restore it, and create beauty where once was ugliness. He can turn us into an unexpected instrument of blessing for others.

Prayer: God, take the blunders of my life and turn them into opportunities to bless others.

The Sewing Machine Puzzle

"Watch out for your fingers." Jane moved her arm to block her ten-year-old son from hovering over the sewing machine where she was stitching a Wandering Foot quilt. "A finger caught under this fast-moving needle would be horrible," she told him.

"But I like to watch," Justin whined. "I'm trying to see what makes the needle go up and down." He leaned close again.

"If you are that interested, I can teach you to sew." Jane deftly guided the material so a red border lay next to the undulating pattern of the Wandering Foot.

"Boys don't sew," Justin protested.

"Boys can make gym bags and golf club covers," Jane challenged her son. "Might come in handy someday to know how to mend a seam in a man's shirt when your wife is too busy."

"I don't want to learn to sew. I want to learn how the machine works."

Jane was getting impatient. "It's very complicated. If it needs work, we take it to a repairman who knows all about sewing machines. Go finish your homework. I need to get this border sewn on because tomorrow my quilt guild is coming. We're going to handquilt this, just like a quilting bee in the old days."

When Justin arrived home from school the next day, he found his mother and a group of women in the living room, seated around a large quilt frame. Mother's blue and white Wandering Foot quilt top was securely fastened in the frame. The women's conversation moved as fast as their needles.

The fascinating sewing machine stood all by itself in the family room. At the base of the machine, a screwdriver gleamed in the light of a nearby lamp as if to beckon him.

Justin picked up the screwdriver and ran his hand over the machine. His hand stopped at the door to the left and above the needle. He fingered the door and it opened. Inside, an amazing crank seemed attached to the arm that made the needle go up and down. Justin turned the wheel on the other side of the machine like he'd seen his mother do, and watched in delight as the needle went up and down. He pulled on a metal plate under where the needle went and discovered interesting gears and lots of screws everywhere. He placed the screwdriver into one. It fit!

Pleased, Justin set about to learn how the machine worked. He was so intrigued, he didn't notice when the ladies left. Then he heard his mother clanking pans to pre-pare dinner.

He hurried to put the machine back together, but he was confused about what went where. He hadn't realized how many pieces he had disassembled. He dropped some screws in his haste to try to make everything all right. He was on the floor picking them up when he heard the scream.

Justin froze.

His mother was standing over him and pointing at the machine. Her mouth was working but she didn't seem to find any words.

Justin crawled under the sewing machine table. "I didn't mean to hurt the sewing machine. I just wanted to see how it worked." His voice trembled. "I'm sorry. Do you think the machine man could fix it? I'll give you my piggy bank."

Several weeks later, after an expensive trip to the repairman with all the parts in a box, the sewing machine sat once again restored to its place in the family room. Even when Jane had a project laid out on the machine, Justin gave it a respectful distance.

 ## The Master Pattern

Restore us, O God, our savior. Put an end to your anger against us.

Psalm 85:4

No matter what mistakes of judgment we make, no matter what errors of action we commit, God is willing to restore us to himself. When we acknowledge we've been wrong and tell him we are sorry, God forgives us. We do well to admit our mistakes to people we have harmed, asking their forgiveness and offering to make restitution wherever possible. Humbling ourselves can go a long way to bringing about restoration; wherever we mess up, God will help us make matters right.

Prayer: God, forgive me for the times I've made mistakes which brought trouble to others. Forgive me for the times I've harmed you and your kingdom. Restore me to a right relationship with you and with the people around me.

Wandering Dog's Feet

"I want a dog," Ava pleaded. She had learned from her many previous requests for a dog that whining worked against her, but her mother didn't succumb to Ava's smile and practiced cheery voice.

"No," Rene told her daughter. "No dog. A dog is too much work for this busy household." Rene finished packing her Wandering Foot quilt into her satchel to finish at her Saturday quilting class.

"Please, please," Ava begged, folding her hands together as if praying. "Sometimes I even dream about a doggy living here."

"I'm running late for class. We'll talk about why a dog isn't a good idea tomorrow." Rene gave her daughter a kiss. "Maybe Daddy will read you a doggy bedtime story while I'm gone."

That evening, Rene returned home to a question from her husband. "Do you know what Ava prayed for when she went to bed tonight?" Tony asked.

"Don't tell me she's still asking for a dog?"

"Passionately. You mean she's prayed for a dog before?"

"Night after night," Rene said. "Tomorrow I'll explain to her again why it isn't a good idea."

Before she could do so, however, there was Sunday school the next day. Ava's teacher and neighbor, Mrs. Smith, had invited Ava to have lunch at her house after church services.

"You know she's been praying for a dog?" Mrs. Smith asked Rene before they left for lunch.

"We aren't buying a dog," Rene said, turning to hug her daughter. Rene lifted Ava's chin. "Your teacher's house is just around the corner so you may walk home after lunch."

Tony and Rene were relaxing on the front porch with the Sunday paper after lunch when Ava ran up the steps.

"Mama, Daddy, look what God sent me. I prayed and prayed and God answered my prayers. He sent me a dog." A bedraggled dog followed Ava up the porch steps. He wagged his tail, thumping Ava's leg. She leaned over and smoothed the dirty black hair on his back. "We asked all the houses around Mrs. Smith's house, and he doesn't belong to anyone. I'm naming him Askie."

"Askie?" Tony raise an eyebrow. "What kind of a name is that?"

"I asked God and he sent me a dog, so I'll call him Askie."

"Oh, my." Rene was speechless.

"Here, Askie, fetch." Ava threw a stick and the thin, scruffy looking dog ran after it with Ava close behind.

"What a mangy looking animal," Rene said. "I really don't want a dog."

"I really don't want to crush Ava's faith either," Tony said, watching their daughter and the dog run around the yard.

"Me neither." Rene sighed. "I guess we'd better get the vet to check out Askie and make sure he doesn't have worms or something."

Not only did Askie stay, a lively symbol of God answering prayer, but he appropriated the Wandering Foot quilt Rene had finished only the day before his arrival. The quilt made a nice soft bed.

When her mother explained why it would be better if the dog didn't sleep on her new quilt because of the superstition around its name, Ava dismissed the concern. "He won't wander off no matter what the quilt is named, Mama. God sent me a dog who loves me."

Askie licked Ava's chin.

 ## The Master Pattern

O LORD, listen to my prayer.
Open your ears to hear my urgent requests.
Answer me because you are faithful and
    righteous.

Psalm 143:1

Isn't it amazing that God listens to our prayers? He actually grants us the joy and privilege to participate in the kingdom of God through prayer. Whether our prayers are desperate ones born out of dire need, or merely the desires of a girlish heart, God cares about what is on our minds. He delights when we include him and converse with him about what we are thinking. He knows exactly the best way to answer our prayers and the best time to send his answers.

Whether we receive the answer we desire at the time we want or not, let's always rejoice and be glad because he hears our cries.

He's pleased that we pray, and he knows how to work faith into our souls.

Prayer: God, grant me the simple faith of a little child. Allow me to thankfully recognize your answers to my prayers even when they aren't in the form I requested. Help my faith to grow and mature.

Acknowledgments

Quilters are amazingly generous people. I wish to thank all the lovely quilters who shared their quilting stories with me.

Thanks also to Nancy Gloss, the owner of Calico Patch, a quilt shop; and Mary Frances Ballard and Karen DiMarino, who graciously supplied me with research resources and patiently answered my questions.

I give thanks for the faithful band of prayer partners who have prayed for me and this project. I'm grateful for you all.

I also wish to thank my son Andrew Tatem for carefully evaluating the manuscript with suggestions to improve it.

About the Author

Mary Tatem loves quilting, but she doesn't come from a long line of quilters. She jokes that she made her first stitches on clumsily fashioned doll clothes. The first quilt she completed, after learning the art from a women's group, was for her daughter's wedding in 1982. She's been quilting ever since and has completed a number of Sunbonnet quilts for her grandchildren.

She does come from a long line of women skilled in the textile arts. As a child, Mary carded wool for her grandmother, who made simple quilts by sewing two sheets of white muslin together and using homegrown, carded wool for the middle layer. Yarn, sewn through all the layers at intervals and tied with knots, held the three layers in place. Mary remembers sleeping under those warm coverlets throughout childhood.

When not quilting, or writing about it, Mary hosts a biweekly home Bible study, works with her church's singles groups, and provides premarital counseling. She's been a

Sunday school teacher, a Girl Scout leader, and a sponsor for mothers' groups. She speaks on relationships and how to grow spiritually, and she leads writing workshops.

Mary has published five other books, including the best-selling *The Quilt of Life: A Patchwork of Devotional Thoughts*. Her feature articles have appeared in a variety of magazines.

Mary lives in Newport News, Virginia, with her husband; they have four adult children and fifteen grandchildren, who all love beautiful threads.

Visit the author's website at www.marytatem.com.

About the Illustrator

Kevin Ingram, a professional illustrator and graphic artist, works in a wide range of media, from oil to computer-aided design. Now at work on his own publishing project, he specializes in portraiture and freelance work for the publishing industry.

While he's never put needle to a quilting square, Kevin is a keeper of a family quilt story: "My great-grandmother Maggie met with a group of ladies at a quilting guild in a rural Indiana church. Every week, around large quilting frames, they sewed and shared 'community news' (yes, gossip). After a few hours they would pack up their needles and thread, stow the frames, and go their separate ways. All except Maggie. Because one of her friends in the guild was truly horrible at stitching, and Maggie knew the woman's work would never hold, she stayed behind to rip out all her friend's work and restitch the squares. Maggie would never embarrass her friend, and none of the other women found out her quirky secret."

One of Maggie's quilts is depicted in an illustration for this book.

For more of Ingram's work, check out his website at www.kicreate.com.

More Inspirational and Heartwarming Stories of Faith and Comfort

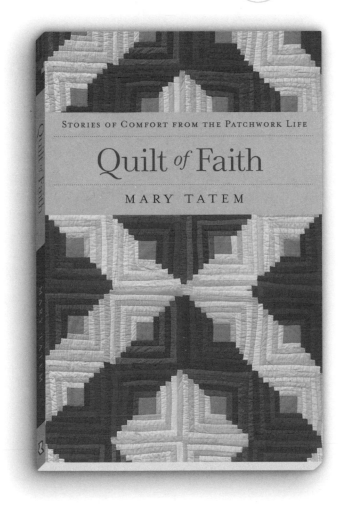

STORIES OF COMFORT FROM THE PATCHWORK LIFE

Quilt *of* Faith

MARY TATEM

Revell
a division of Baker Publishing Group
www.RevellBooks.com

Available wherever books are sold.

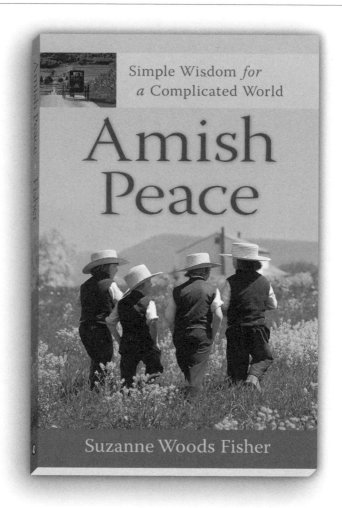